Policy and Research on Gender Equality: An Overview

Gender Equality, Volume 1

Milos Kankaras

Published by Dr. Miloš Kankaraš, 2022.

POLICY AND RESEARCH ON GENDER EQUALITY: AN OVERVIEW

First edition. July 11, 2022.

Copyright © 2022 Milos Kankaras.

ISBN: 979-8223639930

Written by Milos Kankaras.

Policy and Research on Gender Equality: An Overview

Dr Miloš Kankaraš

Executive summary

Key frameworks and definitions of gender equality

There is a great deal of similarity and overlap across numerous existing definitions of gender equality. In a nutshell, gender equality can be thought of as a situation in which individuals, groups and institutions consistently treat human beings in the same way irrespective of their gender. Gender equality is about equal conditions (opportunities, treatment, responsibilities, rights, valuing), not equal results/outcomes. Gender equality recognises differences between women and men and between different groups of women and men but asks them to be treated and valued as equal irrespective of any such differences. Gender equality is understood as a fundamental human right and a multidimensional phenomenon that must be ensured across various domains or spheres of personal, group and institutional life.

Key actors

There is a diverse set of stakeholders and actors involved globally in various gender equality issues. The most important ones are international inter-governmental institutions, representing "standard setters" and custodian agencies for the UN's Sustainable Development Goals. The development of a comprehensive architecture of institutions dedicated either solely or partly to promoting women's empowerment and gender equality was exceptionally robust in the recent decades, mainly following the emergence of a robust international policy framework on gender equality.

A growing number of international non-governmental organisations is either solely or partially focused on gender equality, leading to the increased number of private-public partnerships. Civil society organisations also connect countries to technical and financial resources and advocate for gender equality. Many other stakeholders also play an essential role in gender equality, including academic institutions, think tanks, media, influential individuals, etc.

Legal frameworks of gender equality

*Over the last century, especially after the Second World War, a robust international framework for women's rights has developed. The international community has drafted several policy platforms and legal instruments to help countries worldwide achieve gender equality and women's empowerment. The most important international treaties are the **Convention on the Elimination of all Forms of Discrimination Against Women (1979)** with 189 country signatories and the **Beijing Platform for Action** (1995). They clearly state the principle that the rights of women and girls are an inalienable, integral and indivisible part of universal human rights. The United Nations' **Sustainable Development Goals (SDGs)**, a benchmark to be globally reached by 2030, also aim, among their other goals, to "achieve gender equality and empower all women and girls". On top of these international frameworks, each country has its own legislative and institutional framework that regulates various aspects of gender equality.*

Dimensions of gender equality used in the international empirical research

Whether it is a predominantly legal, empirical or political framework, gender equality is always a multidimensional construct. The number and type of these dimensions vary across frameworks, both in granularity and content. Nevertheless, there are also many similarities and overlaps. Some of the most commonly mentioned dimensions or domains of gender equality are economic conditions, health, education, and political participation. Often included domains are also: violence against women, disaggregated financial aspects (work, money and wealth/ownership), and disaggregated political aspects (political power, economic power, equal treatment by a government, legal frameworks, etc.). Less often mentioned aspects of gender equality are those related to social norms and values, environment, intersecting inequalities, media, deeper-rooted power structures, etc. Most frameworks point out the inter-dependability of various dimensions and their interaction with other related aspects.

Empirical evidence on gender equality across identified dimensions

Many governmental, non-governmental, academic institutions and coalitions are actively involved in empirical research on gender equality, either as their primary subject or as one of their topics of interest. The state of global evidence on gender equality is characterised by the significant differences in data availability and quality across domains and the increasing pace of data gathering and analysis in recent decades. Recent years also show marked improvement in the coordination of the empirical efforts across various organisations, spearheaded by empirical data gathering around the UN's SDGs. Notably, several private-public partnerships have emerged, whose main contribution is invigorating efforts to produce better-quality data and coordinate these efforts across various governmental and non-governmental actors and stakeholders.

Gaps in empirical evidence on Gender Equality

In cases when gender equality data is not available or does not accurately capture the realities of women's and men's lives, funding is inefficiently allocated, and policies may not meet the needs of the people they should serve. A lack of gender-disaggregated data is one of the critical factors preventing faster progress in this area. For example, we currently lack data for 80 % of the gender equality indicators across the SDGs. Even a few years ago, only 37 % of the 126 countries surveyed by the UN Statistics Division had a coordinating body to ensure the collection of sex-disaggregated statistics.

Although the gender data gap is sometimes referred to as a single, homogeneous issue, it comprises several related aspects that are jointly contributing to its size and severity. Apart from the unavailability of data sources, these include compromised data quality, i.e., insufficient reliability and validity of obtained data. Other frequent constraints are lack of adherence to international/national data standards, low recency, lack of trend data, constraints in cross-national comparability, etc. These issues vary in their prominence across domains resulting in vastly different sizes and structures of data gaps across various aspects of gender equality. And while progress on these issues has been made, especially over the last decade, much work still needs to be done to close these data gaps.

Final remarks on the state of empirical evidence in the area of gender equality

Measurability should not subdue the principle of data relevance

The critical question that is missing in most of the reviewed discussions on the empirical evidence in the gender equality domain is the **relevance** *of the selected indicators of gender equality in describing the real-life manifestation and lived experiences of gender relations. For example, it is all too often assumed that the 54 gender-specific indicators in the UN's SDG framework account for the entirety of the gender equality aspects, or at least for the majority of them. But it is enough, for instance, to note that the only SDG indicator of gender equality in the area of digital technology and, indeed, the technology as a whole is whether or not a person owns a mobile phone.*

What makes the problem worse in this sense is that there is a clear bias towards the inclusion of measurable quantitative indicators. There are obvious, practical reasons for doing this. The indicators that can be more easily quantified and measured allow easier, cheaper, more standardised data gathering and analyses, comparisons, and index constructions. However, although quantitative indicators often validly reflect some aspects of the relevant reality, they are not comprehensive in accounting for the entirety of lived experiences of gender inequality. One could even claim that precisely those difficult-to-capture moments and subjective experiences in daily lives are crucial aspects of gender inequality as perceived or experienced by women and girls worldwide. The solution is not to stop collecting quantitative data but rather to be aware of the gaps in these data and their shortcomings and translate this awareness into a correct and honest interpretation of such data. Likewise, much more needs to be done to capture the lived experiences of women and girls in the full complexity and myriad of aspects.

The widest data gap of all is where it could matter the most

It is essential to realise that the empirical data on gender equality is part of a broader system or network, sometimes referred to as the data value chain. This data chain is a process in which data go through four stages: collection, publication, uptake and impact. Many stakeholders cover multiple stages of the data value chain, but most focus on collecting or publishing data. Fewer stakeholders work to increase the uptake of gender data among users, and even fewer focus on the impacts of gender data to directly improve the lives of women and girls.

This situation calls for more efforts in the last stages of the data value chain, especially in the 'Impact' stage, where the fewest stakeholders are engaged. After all, the value and effectiveness of all stages directly depend on the successful administration of this last stage. Furthermore, it is precisely in this final stage where the most significant gender data gap of all might occur, although it is also the least discussed. In particular, there is very little solid empirical evidence on which policy initiatives work, which do not work and which factors and contextual characteristics contribute to or influence policy outcomes. Without such empirical knowledge, we are very far from translating our available gender data into effective policy action.

Abbreviations and acronyms

AWID The Association for Women's Rights in Development

BMGF Bill and Melinda Gates Foundation

BPA The Beijing Platform for Action

CEDAW Convention on the Elimination of all Forms of Discrimination Against Women

CIFF Children's Investment Fund Foundation

CSW The United Nations Commission on the Status of Women

DHS Demographic and Health Surveys

ECOSOC Economic and Social Council

EIGE European Institute for Gender Equality

EU European Union

EWL European Women's Lobby

FAO The Food and Agriculture Organization of the UN

FGE The Foundation for Gender Equality

FGM/C Female genital mutilation/cutting

GDI Gender Development Index

GEM Global Entrepreneurship Monitor

GII Gender Inequality Index

IAEG The Inter-agency and Expert Group

IAW International Alliance of Women

ICRW The International Center for Research on Women

IFC International Finance Corporation

ILO International Labour Organisation

ITU International Telecommunication Union

IWDA International Women's Development Agency

LDCs Least developed countries

LMICs Lower-middle-income countries

MDGs Millennium Development Goals

NGOs Non-governmental organisations

OECD Organisation for Economic Cooperation and Development

PARIS21 Partnership in Statistics for Development in the 21st Century

PPPs Public-private partnerships

SDGs The Sustainable Development Goals

SIGI Social Institutions and Gender Index

STBF The Susan Thompson Buffet Foundation

TTI The Think Tank Initiative

UIS The UNESCO Institute for Statistics

UN United Nations

UNDP United Nations Development Program

UNECE United Nation Economic Commission for Europe

UNESCAP The United Nations Economic and Social Commission
for Asia and the Pacific

UNODC United Nations Office on Drugs and Crime

VDPA The Vienna Declaration and Programme of Action

WEDO Women's Environment and Development Organization

WEF World Economic Forum

WHO World Health Organization

1. Introduction

Gender equality is a fundamental human right. It is also a foundation of a prosperous, fair and equitable society that allows for sustainable, inclusive and environmentally conscious living. Gender equality is critical for ensuring that men and women can contribute fully at home, at work and in public life, for the betterment of communities and societies at large.

Ensuring that modern societies are places of equality and are free from discrimination is essential for achieving the Sustainable Development Goals (SDGs). Meeting SDG 5, gender equality and the empowerment of all women and girls, for example, demands the elimination of violence and an end to harmful practices and ensuring women have access to economic resources. It also assumes promoting shared responsibility for the provision of unpaid care and domestic work, which falls disproportionately on women's shoulders.

However, one of the key factors in the successful fulfilment of SDGs is the availability of relevant and valid data. Indeed, some consider the underachievement of the United Nations Millennium Development Goals (MDGs) - including MDG 5, to improve maternal health due to the lack of indicators to track progress (Leadership Council of the Sustainable Development Solutions Network 2015). And although SDGs that have replaced the MDGs have more indicators than any previous global development goals, we are still currently lacking data for 80 per cent of the gender equality indicators across the SDGs (UN Women, 2017).

Gaps in gender data and the lack of trend data make it difficult to monitor progress for women and girls. Unless gender is mainstreamed into international and national statistical strategies and prioritized in data collection, gender data scarcity and gaps will persist. Investment in national statistical capacity is central to improving data coverage, quality, and timeliness for monitoring gender equality and the SDGs. Equally important is making sure that data represent the lived reality of women and girls in all their diversity.

This report aims to overview the global state of gender equality policy and research. It describes the main actors and stakeholders in the field and outlines the development of international legal and policy frameworks on gender equality and related issues. The report also introduces key frameworks and perspectives on gender equality and briefly discusses the main aspects and dimensions identified across various approaches. The report also examines the main sources of empirical evidence, international analytical studies and indicators, and data depositories. Finally, the report concludes with the chapter outlining key limitations and empirical data gaps in inter nationally available empirical evidence.

2. Key frameworks and definitions of gender equality

Numerous institutions and policy and academic works have developed their conceptualisations of gender equality. Here we will list several definitions of gender equality from the key institutional players in the world and then shortly discuss the critical aspects of their gender equality conceptualisations.

UN Women[1] (2015):

"**Gender equality** means equal opportunities, rights and responsibilities for women and men, girls and boys. Equality does not mean that women and men are the same but that women's and men's opportunities, rights and responsibilities do not depend on whether they are born, or they identify themselves as female or male. It implies that the interests, needs and priorities of both women and men are taken into consideration."

UNICEF[2]:

"Gender equality means that women and men, girls and boys have equal conditions, treatment and opportunities for realising their full potential, human rights and dignity, and for contributing to (and benefitting from) e will become the same but that women's and men's rights, responsibilities and opportunities will not depend on whether they are born male or female."

---

1. https://www.undp.org/publications/inclusive-electoral-processes-guide-electoral-management-bodies-promoting-gender

2. https://www.unicef.org/rosa/media/1761/file/
Gender%20glossary%20of%20terms%20and%20concepts%20.pdf

EU – European Institute for Gender Equality[3] (EIGE):

"Gender equality refers to the equal rights, responsibilities and opportunities of women and men and girls and boys. Equality does not mean that women and men will become the same but that women's and men's rights, responsibilities and opportunities will not depend on whether they are born male or female. Gender equality implies that the interests, needs and priorities of both women and men are taken into consideration, recognising the diversity of different groups of women and men. Gender equality is not a women's issue but should concern and fully engage men as well as women. Equality between women and men is seen both as a human rights issue and as a precondition for, and indicator of, sustainable people-centred development."

"Unequal access to and control over the various material and non-material resources and assets of the society. In all societies the woman's role is the inferior one in the relationship. There is still no country in the world where women have equal access to power and decision-making, and to decent and well-paid jobs."

UN (Convention on the Elimination of all Forms of Discrimination Against Women - CEDAW[4]):

"Any distinction, exclusion or restriction made on the basis of sex which has the effect or purpose of impairing or nullifying the recognition, enjoyment or exercise by women, irrespective of their marital status, on the basis of equality of men and women, of human rights and fundamental freedoms in the political, economic, social, cultural, civil or any other field."

There is a great deal of similarity and overlap across existing definitions of gender equality. Here is their summary:

---

3. https://www.un.org/womenwatch/osagi/conceptsanddefinitions.htm

4. https://endcorporalpunishment.org/human-rights-law/cedaw/

- In a nutshell, gender equality can be thought of as a situation in which individuals, groups and institutions consistently treat human beings in the same way irrespective of their gender.

- Gender equality is about equal conditions (opportunities, treatment, responsibilities, rights, and valuing).

- Gender equality is not equality of results/outcomes (stated explicitly in some definitions).

- Gender equality recognises differences between women and men but asks that they are treated and valued as equal irrespective of any such differences.

- Gender equality recognises the diversity of different groups of women and men and assumes that they should all be treated equally irrespective of their gender.

- Gender equality is perceived as a fundamental human right.

- Gender equality is a multidimensional phenomenon that must be achieved in various fields or spheres of the personal, group and institutional life.

- Non-binary identities are not mentioned explicitly in the definitions given by the crucial institutional players in the field.

3. Key actors

Many stakeholders are involved in various aspects of gender equality issues and policies. For example, in gender equality data, eight broad groups of stakeholders are identified, each comprising a set of institutions and actors at national and international levels (**Figure 1**).

Figure 1: Main actors in the area of the national and international data on gender equality

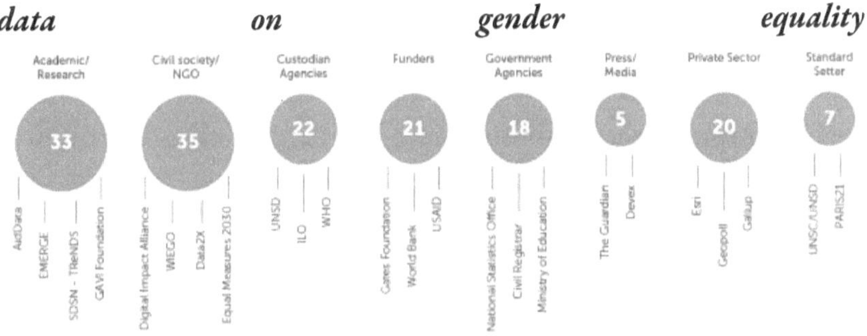

Source: Open Data Watch, 2021

International Inter-governmental organisations

Many international inter-governmental institutions are involved in the issue of gender equality and women's rights, including "standard setters" and custodian agencies for the UN's Sustainable Development Goals, such as the UN System of organisations. These remain crucial in setting standards and supporting data collection and reporting, with the UN Statistics Division and UN Women playing instrumental roles concerning gender data efforts. However, when it comes to the global state of gender equality, international inter-governmental organizations primarily or partially dealing with gender equality are the most important actors in the field. That is because they have a global scope of influence and tend to have the most power to change things globally: direct impact on international and national policy-making, most funds, and other resources.

The development of a comprehensive architecture of institutions dedicated either solely or partly to promoting women's empowerment and gender equality was solid in the recent decades, mainly following the emergence of a robust international policy framework on gender equality (discussed in the following section). International and local non-governmental organisations have spearheaded this process. In addition, most countries have created national women's machinery (usually a ministry) to oversee the implementation of country commitments to international obligations, along with particular positions or gender units responsible for incorporating gender in the sector. However, these ministries and units are often under-resourced and lack sufficient capacity (world bank report).

Some of the crucial international inter-governmental organisations working in the area of gender equality are:

- UN Women

- Other UN organisations: UNESCO, UNICEF, WHO, UNSD, UNDP, UNFAO, etc.

- The World Bank: Gender and Development

- OECD: Development Centre & Gender Data Portal

- The World Economic Forum: Global Agenda Council on Gender Parity

- European Institute for Gender Equality (EIGE)

- ILO Gender (Bureau for Gender Equality)

- International Finance Corporation (IFC) Women in Business Program

Each of these organisations has its work program in the area, collects its data, produces its own (progress) reports, and is usually (co)custodian for some SDG indicators. The following chapters of this report will give more information about their work.

Academia

Academic scholars have dedicated a considerable effort towards understanding gender equality, its determinants, consequences, and the appropriate actions and policies to advance women's equality. These include academics from related disciplines and the relatively recently established interdisciplinary fields of gender and human rights studies. As a result, research on gender equality has advanced especially rapidly in the past decades, with a steady increase in publications on mainstream topics related to women in education and the workforce, and on other emerging issues. The publications cover many topics, ranging from women's education and human capital and role in society to their appointment in firms' top-ranked positions and performance implications.

Academic literature has highlighted that gender issues and their economic and social ramifications are complex topics involving many possible antecedents and outcomes. Diverse bodies of literature (e.g., business, economics, development studies, sociology and psychology) approach the problem of achieving gender equality from different perspectives – often addressing specific and narrow aspects. That sometimes leads to a lack of clarity about how various issues, circumstances, and solutions may be related to precipitating or mitigating gender inequality or its effects.

A recent meta-analysis of academic research on gender equality has found that most research has been done on work-related issues. In particular, the five most researched topics are compensation, role, education, decision-making and career progression, exceeding others in prevalence (mentioned more often), diversity (mentioned in more other topics) and connectivity (more central to the discourse of gender equality) (**Figure 2**). The topics that follow – hiring, performance, behaviour, organisation and human capital – are also directly or indirectly related to women in the workforce.

Figure 2: Most researched topics in the academic literature on gender equality

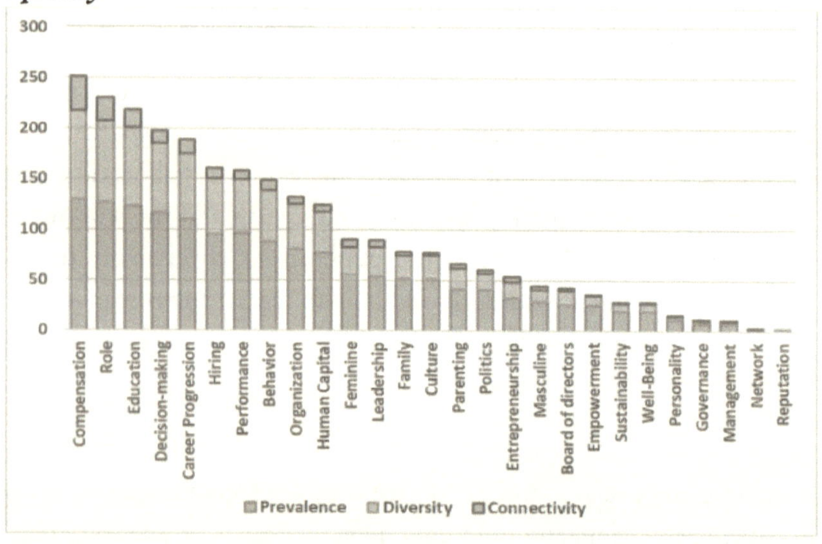

Source: Belingheri et al., (2021). https://doi.org/10.1371/journal.pone.0256474

However, the level of interest in any of the identified academic research topics is far from static. Analysis of the changes in interest in the 27 identified topics of scholarly research on gender equality has found that scholars' focus is shifting and that new topics are constantly emerging (**Figure 3**). For example, interest in the dominant subject of compensation seems to be losing momentum while interest in performance, organisations, leadership, entrepreneurship, board of directors and sustainability is gaining momentum, especially in the last few years. It is also interesting to note "feminine" topic (defined as "female characteristics") has been consistently one of the most important over the last two decades. However, its importance fluctuated over the periods of 3-4 years.

Figure 3: Emerging topics in academic research

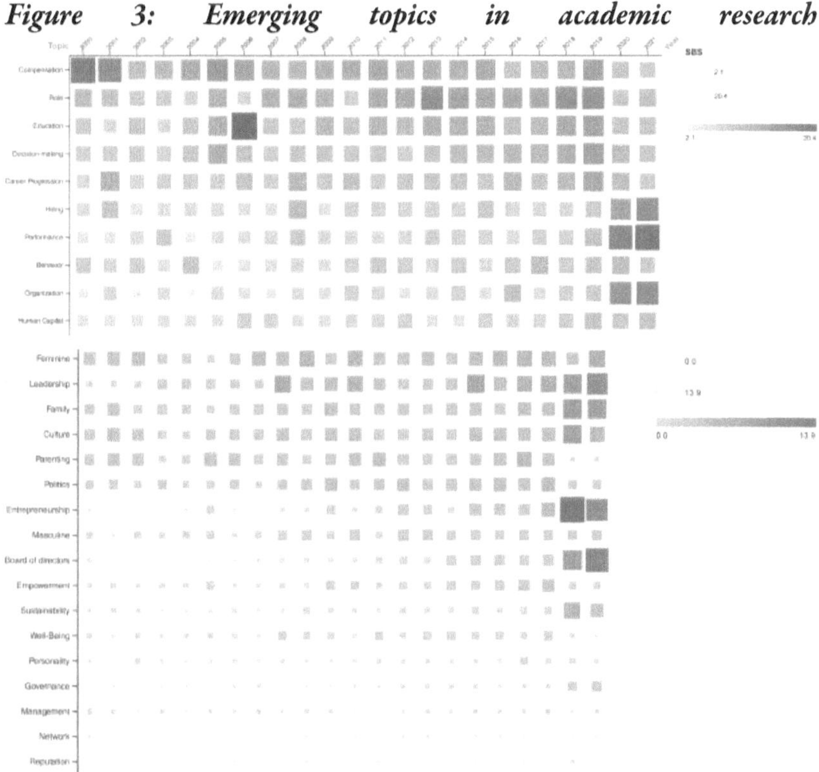

Source: *Belingheri et al., (2021). https://doi.org/10.1371/journal.pone.0256474*

The overview of the academic literature also shows some critical gaps. At the highest level of abstraction, there is an abundance of studies on identifying issues related to gender inequalities and imbalances in the workforce and society. Literature has thoroughly examined the (unconscious) biases, barriers, stereotypes, and discriminatory behaviours women face due to their gender. At the same time, fewer studies discuss or demonstrate effective solutions to overcome gender bias (Belingheri et al., 2021). That is partly due to the relative ease in studying the status quo instead of studying changes in the status quo. However, we observed a shift in the more recent years towards solution-seeking in this domain.

Non-governmental Organisations (NGOs)

Over the past few decades, a growing number of non-governmental organisations at both international and national levels have been involved in various aspects of the gender equality policy landscape. Furthermore, the active participation of NGOs is increasingly seen as a critical element in the work of different multi-stakeholder bodies and initiatives, such as the United Nations Commission on the Status of Women (CSW) (UN CSW, 2013). In particular, UN Women facilitates the participation of accredited NGOs in the meetings of the CSW, allowing for their active role and contribution to the annual sessions of the CSW. In Europe, the European Commission organises bi-annual meetings with the Social Platform, the largest network of European rights- and value-based civil society organisations working in the social sector. These meetings discuss current policy issues with non-governmental organisations (NGOs). Likewise, various national and international governmental institutions provide funding for NGOs' activities in the area of gender equality. For example, under the *Rights, equality and citizenship programme*, the European Commission funds[1] a range of European NGO networks, including the European Network of Equality Bodies (Equinet).

NGOs actively shape the current global policy framework on women's empowerment and gender equality: the Beijing Declaration and

---

1. https://ec.europa.eu/info/policies/justice-and-fundamental-rights/combatting-discrimination/tackling-discrimination/non-governmental-organisations-fighting-against-discrimination_en

Platform for Action. They continue to play an essential role in holding international and national leaders accountable for their commitments in the Platform for Action.

In the following paragraphs, we will list some of the most important international NGOs in the area of gender equality.

Association for Women's Rights in Development[2]

The Association for Women's Rights in Development (AWID) is an international non-governmental organization working to achieve gender equality and women's human rights worldwide. The organization supports the gender justice movements to become driving forces in oppression. The AWID closely works with activists and policymakers worldwide to influence gender policies and practices. It facilitates dialogue and strategies on critical issues by connecting actors to share their knowledge, experiences and ideas on relevant topics. It mobilizes gender equality movements to support collective actions with feminist causes. It works with activists to build support networks of solidarity on protection and wellbeing and works with historically oppressed communities. Last but not least, the AWID advocates for corporate accountability and tax justice to achieve equitable distribution of wealth.

Womankind Worldwide[3]

Womankind Worldwide is an international non-governmental organization for women's rights that works in solidarity and equal partnership with women's rights organizations and movements to transform women's lives. The organisation's vision is a just world where the rights of all women are respected, realized and valued. Currently, Womankind Worldwide works with women's rights organizations and

---

2. https://www.awid.org/

3. https://www.womankind.org.uk/

movements in Ethiopia, Kenya, Nepal, Uganda and Zimbabwe, advocating for international agencies and governments to promote and protects women's rights.

Together with its local partners, Womankind Worldwide helps women and girls transform their lives by providing shelters to escape violence. It also implements projects with community leaders to help women talk about what they want to change in their communities and how to achieve that. It also supports the women's rights movements by providing technical support, funding opportunities and advocacy platform. The organization also uses its expertise to influence policy changes and ensure that women's rights are placed at the heart of the international agenda.

<u>Plan International</u>[4]

Plan International is a global development human rights and humanitarian organization working to advance children's rights and equality for girls. It closely works with young people, children, and communities to tackle the root causes of discrimination against girls, vulnerability, and exclusion. It enables them to respond and prepare for adversity and practice. Plan International influences policies and procedures at local, national and global levels using knowledge, experience and reach.

Some of the core objectives of Plan International are achieving gender equality, promoting gender justice and fostering an inclusive society. The organization confronts and challenges human rights violations and discrimination based on gender, stereotypes and unequal power relations between women, men, boys and girls to promote rights and gender equality. In addition, plan International fosters a culture that encompasses its commitment to gender equality and adoption of good practices, positive attitudes and inclusion.

---

4. https://plan-international.org/

<u>Women for Women International[5]</u>

Women for Women International is an international women's rights organization that supports the most marginalized women in countries affected by war and conflict. The organization conducts projects that enable women to earn and save money, influence decisions in their communities and homes, improve their well-being and health and connect to networks for support. So far, the organization has helped more than 478.000 women worldwide to rebuild their lives after the war. In addition, women for Women International uses its voice to call for global attention to women's unique role in advancing peace throughout society.

<u>Equality Now[6]</u>

Equality Now is an international non-governmental organization founded to use legal advocacy to protect and promote the human rights of women and girls. It employs the law to create an equal and just world for women and girls. It attracts global attention to media on individual cases of abuse and uses international human rights law to advocate with policymakers, and puts pressure on national governments to adopt and enforce good laws. Equality now partners up with other organizations to ensure that individual cases are visible on the global agenda.

Equality Now cooperates with individuals, institutions, and coalitions encompassing grassroots activists, survivors, legal reformers, lawyers, service providers, corporations and national and regional women's organizations. It uses the knowledge of these organisations and their connections to local communities to achieve change. It also puts pressure on countries to adopt gender equality laws and holds governments accountable for abuses of such laws.

---

5. https://womenforwomen.org.uk/

6. https://www.equalitynow.org/

Women's Environment and Development Organization[7]

Women's Environment and Development Organization (WEDO) is a global advocacy organization created to promote and protect gender equality, human rights and the integrity of their environment. WEDO facilitates and connects movements to global agendas and, in this way, it ensures the recognition of women's voices and the advancement of women's leadership.

WEDO partners up with like-minded organizations and individuals and engages in advocacy to affect policy processes to ensure women's human rights are respected. It also works on the capacity building and facilitating space for women's political voices at local, national and international levels. Moreover, WEDO builds and maintains knowledge on gender equality, women's rights, sustainable development and environmental issues to ensure effective outreach and information sharing.

PROMUNDO[8]

Promundo is an international organization that promotes gender justice and prevents violence by engaging men and boys in partnership with women, girls, and individuals of all gender identities. It was established in 1997 in Brazil, believing that working with men and boys will contribute to eliminating harmful gender norms and provide solutions to achieve gender equality. So far, Promundo has worked in over 40 countries to prevent violence and advocate for gender equality.

In addition to working with individuals, Promundo conducts campaigns and engages in local activism to build community support and advocate for governments to adopt policies that would reinforce social change. It also creates safe spaces for women and men in

---

7. https://wedo.org/

8. https://promundoglobal.org/

post-conflict settings to heal from trauma, for young people to question gender norms, and for men worldwide to discuss violence, exploitation and benefits of shared decision-making. Through its programs, Promundo has reached nearly 10 million individuals, including over 4.500 health professionals, over 22.000 education professionals, over 1.400 members of the police and military, and almost 300 government officials.

<u>Amnesty International</u>[9]

Amnesty International is a worldwide movement with over 2,2 million members who campaign for internationally recognized human rights for all. Amnesty International strives to improve the Universal Declaration of Human Rights through international solidarity and campaigning on human rights issues. Its mission is to conduct research, generate action, prevent and end grave human rights abuses, and demand justice for those whose rights are abused.

One of the main activities of Amnesty International is the fight against violence against women and advocacy for gender equality. Under its campaign to Stop Violence Against Women, the organization advocates for implementing laws that guarantee access to justice to women who are victims of violence. In addition, it works on empowering women, calls for the adoption of new laws that protect women's rights and demands an end to laws that discriminate against women.

<u>Save the Children</u>[10]

Save the Children is one of the most prominent international NGOs advancing and protecting children's rights in almost 120 countries worldwide. It works in the most disadvantaged local communities

---

9. https://www.amnesty.org/en/

10. https://www.savethechildren.net/

educating them about children's rights. Save the Children seeks to advance gender equality in all aspects of its work, recognizing that gender inequalities create significant barriers for sustainable development.

The organization works to ensure that all its programs identify different needs of all actors, including girls, boys, women and men. The organization also utilizes gender-transformative approaches and supports meaningful and lasting impacts in the lives of children by working with key stakeholders to identify and change the root causes of gender inequality. The organization also advocates for policies that promote gender equality and conducts gender research to find innovative solutions and tackle changes.

International Alliance of Women [11]

International Alliance of Women (IAW) is an international non-governmental organization comprising 41-member organizations involved in promoting the human rights of women and girls globally.

IAW currently works on the relation between gender and economic crisis since the economic recession and the financial crisis threaten gender equality and cause poverty. IAW advocates for equal participation of women at all levels in implementing the policies in the corporate and private sectors so that they can call off the harmful effects these policies pose on women. It also advocates for implementing macro-economic policies that respect gender equality and human rights. IAW implements capacity building on feminist economics to enable its members to act on gender issues.

Human Rights Watch [12]

---

11. https://www.womenalliance.org/

12. https://www.hrw.org/

Human Rights Watch was established in 1978 as a non-governmental human rights organization. Today, its network of experts includes human rights professionals, lawyers, journalists and academics. The organization produces detailed reports on human rights violations and abuses on a global scale. Each year, the organization publishes more than 100 reports on human rights conditions in around 80 countries, followed by extensive local and international media coverage.

The reports and publications of Human Rights Watch also address women's rights. Since its establishment, the organization has broadened and strengthened its work in gender equality and women's rights, bringing a human rights dimension to domestic violence, trafficking, rape, and similar. To achieve its goals, the organization meets with governments, regional institutions, financial institutions and corporations to push for policies that promote human rights and justice around the world.

International Women's Development Agency[13]

International Women's Development Agency (IWDA) is an Australian based non-governmental organization working to directly address poverty and oppression in developing countries and create positive change for women and their communities. So far, IWDA has worked with more than 100 grassroots organizations in developing parts of the world to support and advance women's life choices and well-being and their families.

Currently, IWDA implements projects in the Asia Pacific region, devised and managed by women within their communities. The projects are implemented in Cambodia, Timor Leste, Fiji, Papua New Guinea, Bougainville, Solomon Islands, and Burma. The organization works to achieve gender justice in these communities and equitable growth of people.

---

13. https://iwda.org.au/

Private organisations

While governments and inter-governmental institutions remain the majority funders of the gender equality initiatives, non-traditional donors such as foundations and private companies have also begun taking a more prominent role in the global drive for more equitable societies. Private-sector funders and advocacy networks have also risen in importance in recent years in the field of gender-relevant research and data-gathering initiatives. Furthermore, private-public partnerships between public sector agencies and private sector funders and foundations are increasing in number.

Characteristics of global gender equality phylantropy

Although private funding in gender equality has been rising in recent years, it still accounts for a relatively small proportion of total funds allocated to these issues when considering governmental funding. In particular, according to the OECD survey of Private Philanthropy for Development (2018), foundations included in the study provided a total of USD 3.7 billion to support gender equality in developing countries from 2013 to 2015 (**Figure 4**). Over 2013-15, philanthropic giving for gender equality rose from USD 1.1 billion in 2013 and 2014 to USD 1.5 billion in 2015. That is equivalent to 16% of the three-year total philanthropic giving identified for this period and roughly 4% of gender-marked governments' Official Developmental Assistance (ODA).

Figure 4: Sources and amount of financial support for gender equality in developing countries from 2013 to 2015

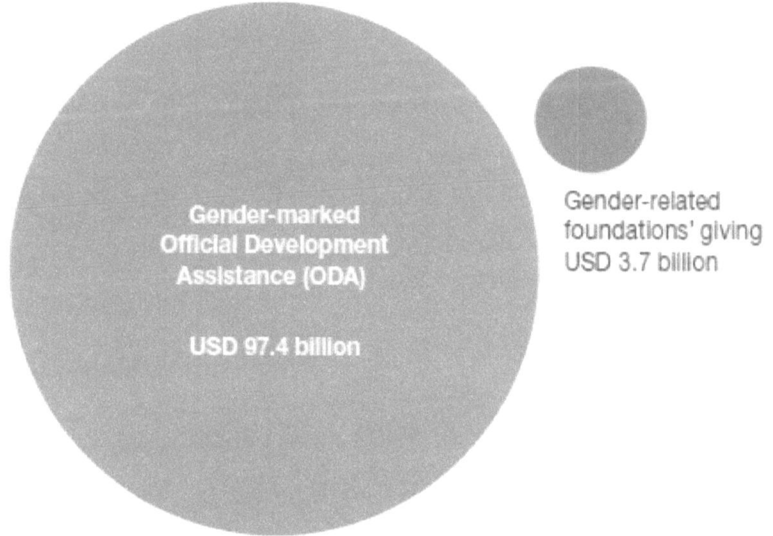

Source: OECD (2018), Survey on Private Philanthropy for Development 2013-15: Data Questionnaire, www.oecd.org/dac/financingsustainable-development/ development-finance-standards/beyond-oda-foundations.htm[14].

Of the 143 foundations included in the OECD survey of global private philanthropy (OECD, 2018b), 48 reported that they provided over USD 1 million in the 2013-15 period, with 22 providing over USD 10 million each. As shown in **Figure 5** below, funding from the Bill and Melinda Gates Foundation (BMGF) accounted for almost half of total gender-related giving (USD 1.6 billion; 43%), followed by the Susan Thompson Buffet Foundation (STBF) (USD 725 million; 19%).

Other foundations donating significant funds to support women and girls are Children's Investment Fund Foundation (CIFF, USD 127 million), Ford Foundation (USD 114 million), Dutch Postcode

---

14. http://www.oecd.org/dac/financingsustainable-development/development-finance-standards/beyond-oda-foundations.htm

Lottery (USD 102 million) and Hewlett Foundation (USD 100 million), representing approximately 3% each.

———————————

Figure   5:   Private   philanthropic   foundations'   donations

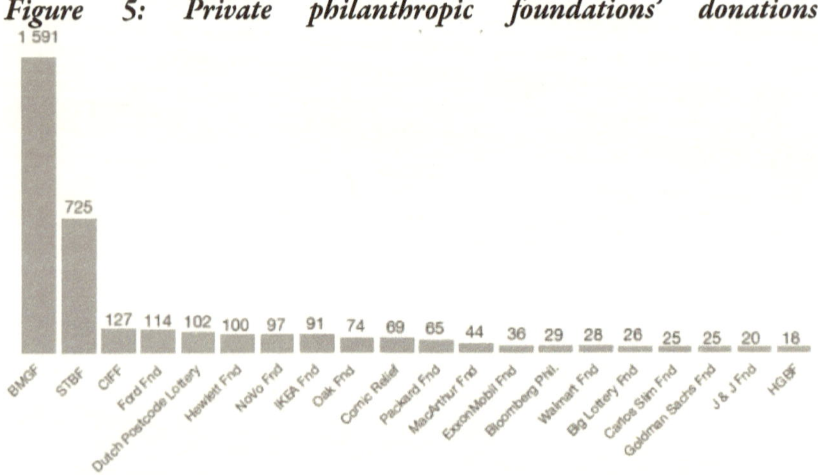

Source: *OECD (2018), Survey on Private Philanthropy for Development 2013-15: Data   Questionnaire,   www.oecd.org/dac/financing-sustainable-development/ development-finance-standards/beyond-oda-foundations.htm[15].*

Looking at the share of foundations' giving dedicated to supporting women and girls reveals that the following seven foundations specialise exclusively on gender (i.e. their support to gender equality constitutes more than 90% of their portfolio), all of them based in North America and Europe: Fondation CHANEL, Goldman Sachs Foundation, NoVo Foundation, Oprah Winfrey Leadership Academy Foundation, Sabanci Foundation, STBF and Walmart Foundation (**Figure 6**).

Figure 6: Share of foundations' giving dedicated to supporting women   and   girls   between   2013-2015

———————————————————————

15. *http://www.oecd.org/dac/financing-sustainable-development/development-finance-standards/beyond-oda-*

  foundations.htm

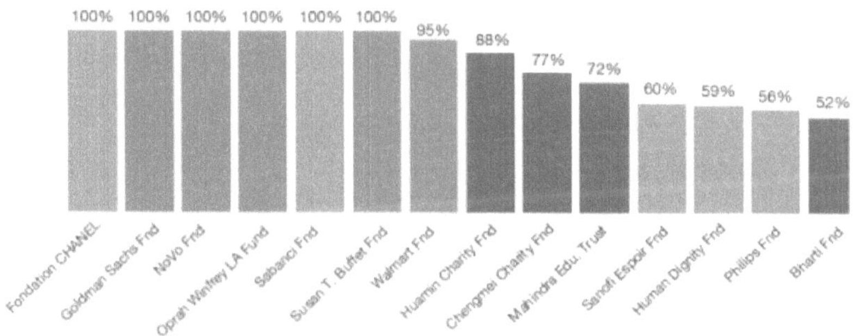

Source: OECD (2018), Survey on Private Philanthropy for Development 2013-15: Data Questionnaire, www.oecd.org/dac/financing-sustainable-development/ development-finance-standards/beyond-oda-foundations.htm[16].

The OECD data on private philanthropy for development shows that, in 2017, 15% of philanthropic funding from 26 of the largest foundations worldwide had the objective of supporting gender equality and women's empowerment, which amounts to USD 0.9 billion for that year (**Figure** 7). In addition, 5% of philanthropic giving have gender equality as a primary objective, and another 11% have gender equality as a secondary objective. Nevertheless, 84% of all charitable flows identified in the recent 2017 survey update were not targeted or identified as addressing goals of gender equality.

Figure 7: Philanthropic funding with gender objective

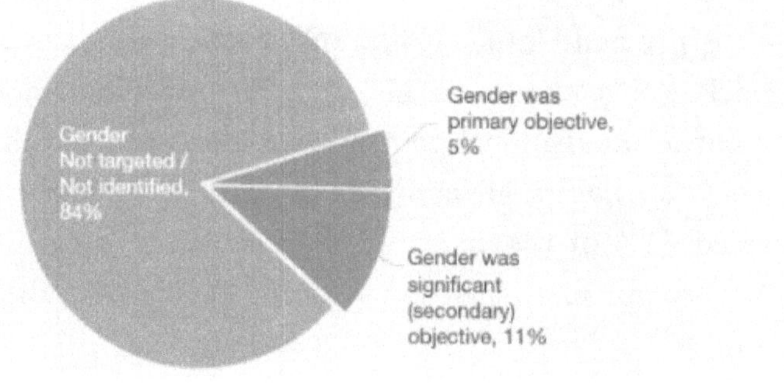

---

16. *http://www.oecd.org/dac/financing-sustainable-development/development-finance-standards/beyond-oda-foundations.htm*

Source: OECD (2019), OECD International Development Statistics: Creditor Reporting System (database), http://www.oecd.org/dac/stats/idsonline.htm.

Philanthropic flows targeting gender equality reported for 2017 allocated 35% of the total giving for gender to Africa, followed by Asia (21%), Latin America (3%) and Europe (0.3%), while almost half of philanthropic giving (41%) had a global or unallocated scope (**Figure 8**).

Figure 8: Global distribution of philanthropic funding for gender

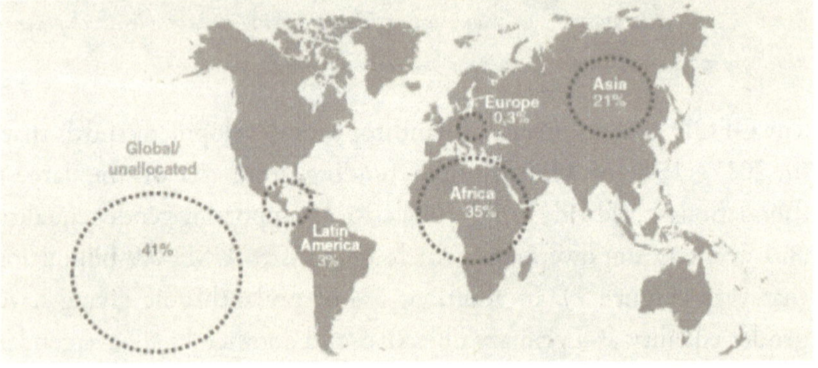

Source: OECD (2019b), OECD International Development Statistics: Creditor Reporting System (database), http://www.oecd.org/dac/stats/idsonline.htm.

In line with the geographic distribution, five of the top ten recipient countries were from the African continent: Nigeria, Ethiopia, Kenya, South Africa and Uganda (**Figure 9**). However, India was the largest beneficiary of gender-related giving (USD 469 million) and the largest recipient of international philanthropic flows overall. That is mainly thanks to significant giving by the BMGF (USD 284 million), who provided 61% of the country's allocated total for gender equality, particularly for reproductive health and family planning (USD 203 million).

Figure 9: Major beneficiaries of gender-related philanthropic donations

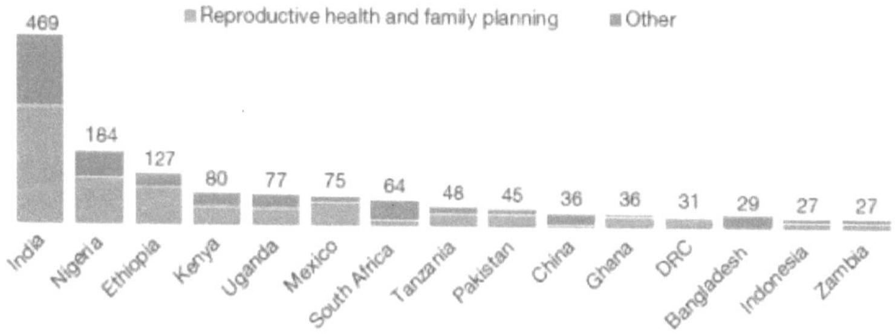

Source: OECD (2018), Survey on Private Philanthropy for Development 2013-15: Data Questionnaire, www.oecd.org/dac/financingsustainable-development/ development-finance-standards/beyond-oda-foundations.htm[17].

In terms of income group, most of the country-allocable gender-related giving went to middle-income countries (64%). In particular, almost half (49%) of foundations' giving went to lower-middle-income countries (LMICs) and only 15% to upper-middle-income countries (UMICs). Surprisingly, only 31% targeted the least developed countries (LDCs) and 5% other low-income countries (LICs). This trend is similar to the 2018 global philanthropy survey (OECD, 2018), although the former targeted slightly more LMICs countries rather than UMICs (**Figure 10**).

---

17. http://www.oecd.org/dac/financingsustainable-development/development-finance-standards/beyond-oda-foundations.htm

Figure 10: Gender-related philanthropy by income group

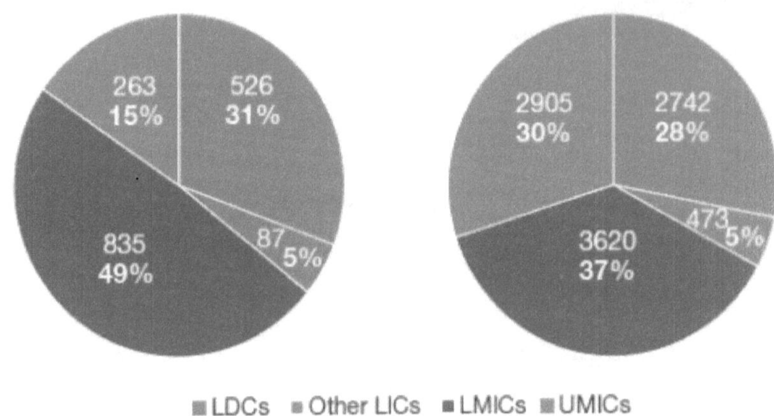

Source: OECD (2018), Survey on Private Philanthropy for Development 2013-15: Data Questionnaire, www.oecd.org/dac/financingsustainable-development/development-finance-standards/beyond-oda-foundations.htm[18].

Health and reproductive health was the most significant sector (73%) to benefit from gender-targeted philanthropic giving, which was in line with the overall philanthropic allocations. In particular, USD 2.18 billion (58% of all giving for gender equality) was dedicated to reproductive health, family planning and population policies, mainly due to the significant donations by BMGF and other large foundations like STBF and CIFF. Other substantial sub-sectors included infectious diseases control (6%) and basic nutrition (4%).

Government and civil society was the second most targeted sector (10%), with activities focused on human rights, democratic participation and civil society development or conflict prevention and resolution. Donating to this sector was more significant for philanthropy supporting gender equality than for global philanthropy for development as a whole. It was directed to women's equality

---

18. http://www.oecd.org/dac/financingsustainable-development/development-finance-standards/beyond-oda-foundations.htm

organisations (3%) and to end violence against women and girls, including female genital mutilation/cutting (FGM/C) (3%). Other significant sectors included education (5%) and agriculture (3%). On the other hand, gender-related funding in some sectors, such as environmental protection or banking and financial services, was found to be very limited (1% each) (**Figure 11**).

Figure 11: Main beneficiaries of gender-related philanthropy by sector

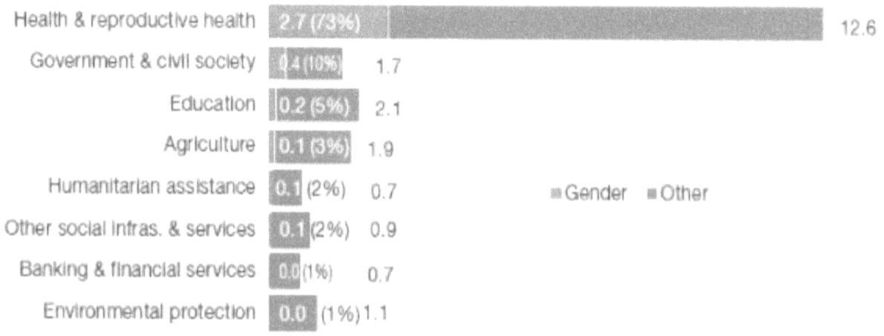

Source: *OECD (2018), Survey on Private Philanthropy for Development 2013-15: Data Questionnaire, www.oecd.org/dac/financing-sustainable-development/development-finance-standards/beyond-oda-foundations.htm[19].*

Almost all philanthropic giving for gender equality (99%) was allocated to intermediary institutions, with less than 1% directly executed by donating foundations. Foundations mainly channel their giving for gender equality through NGOs, civil society, public-private partnerships (PPPs), networks and the for-profit private sector (67% of total gender-related giving). These are followed by university, college or other teaching institutions, research institutes and think-tanks7 (21%); and finally, multilateral organisations (9%) (**Figure 12**).

---

19. http://www.oecd.org/dac/financing-sustainable-development/development-finance-standards/beyond-oda-foundations.htm

Figure   12:   Intermediary   institutions

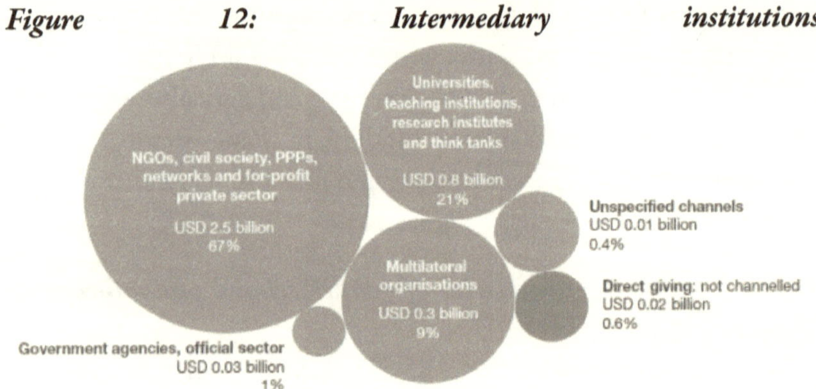

Note: NGOs, civil society, PPPs, networks and the for-profit private sector are grouped since, given the high number of channels stated in responses to the survey, it was not feasible to distinguish which channelling organisations had a not-for-profit or for-profit business model or, for example, to what extent they could qualify as PPPs or networks (OECD, 2018).

Source: OECD (2018), Survey on Private Philanthropy for Development 2013-15: Data Questionnaire, www.oecd.org/dac/financing-sustainable-development/ development-finance-standards/beyond-oda-foundations.htm[20].

Grants are the preferred instrument most gender-related foundations use to allocate their funds, with 94% of them providing grants and 38% providing prizes and awards and matching grants. However, some foundations are increasingly considering new financial tools as an alternative to traditional grantmaking. For instance, 31% provide loans, 19% use guarantees and 13% equity, although these remain limited in terms of volume (**Figure 13**).

---

20. http://www.oecd.org/dac/financing-sustainable-development/development-finance-standards/beyond-oda-foundations.htm

Figure 13: Financial instruments to allocate gender-related funds

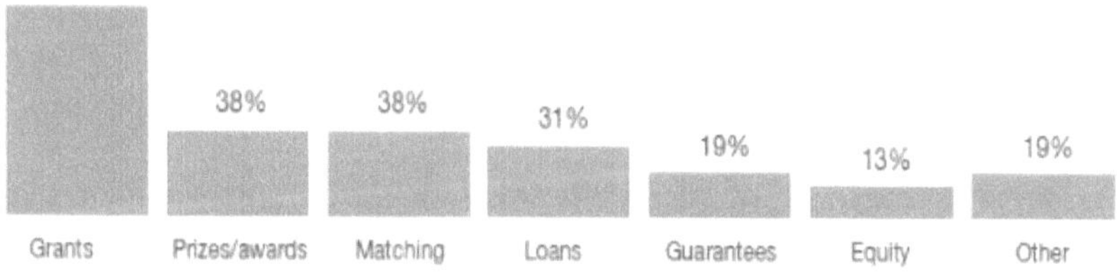

Source: OECD (2018), Survey on Private Philanthropy for Development 2013-15: Qualitative Questionnaire, www.oecd.org/site/netfwd[21].

In addition to financial support, foundations also provide non-financial support to grantees. For example, the majority (75%) of the main foundations working on gender equality provide grantees access to networks, 69% offer strategic consulting, and 31% help them fundraise and develop revenue strategies (**Figure 14**).

Figure   14:   Types   of   non-financial   assistance

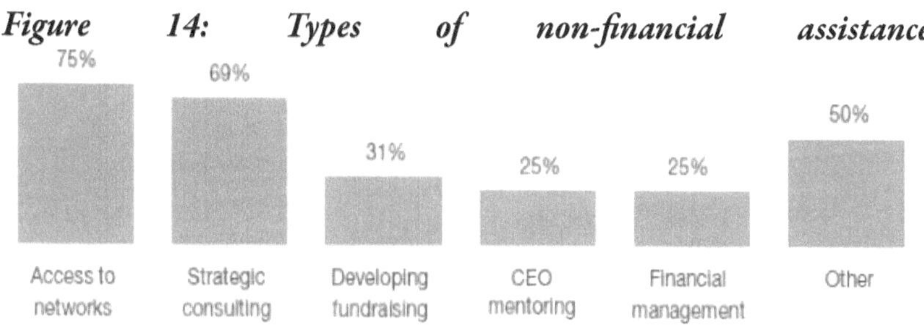

Source: OECD (2018), Survey on Private Philanthropy for Development 2013-15: Qualitative Questionnaire, www.oecd.org/site/netfwd[22].

The engagement period over which funding or support is provided tends to be relatively short. Long-term commitments are pretty rare. The qualitative survey reveals that 75% of the main foundations working on gender equality support initiatives or partners for no longer than five years (**Figure 15**). However, this period is more

---

21. http://www.oecd.org/site/netfwd

22. http://www.oecd.org/site/netfwd

extended than the average for philanthropy for development in general, where 86% of foundations engage for five years or less (OECD, 2018).

Figure 15: Periods of gender-related philanthropic engagement

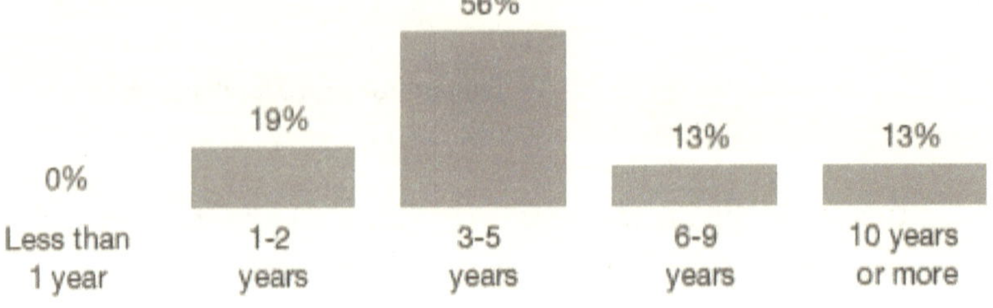

Source: OECD (2018), Survey on Private Philanthropy for Development 2013-15: Qualitative Questionnaire, www.oecd.org/site/netfwd[23].

All surveyed foundations working on gender equality report evaluating their programmes – with almost two-thirds doing it "systematically" and over one-third "sometimes". However, figures are much lower when evaluating their performance as foundations. For example, the OECD survey reveals that 18% of the main foundations working on gender never measure their institutional performance, while only 36% do it "sometimes" and 45% do it "systematically" (**Figure 16**). Nevertheless, results suggest that foundations supporting gender equality, women and girls more regularly evaluate their programs and institutional performance than the foundations reviewed in the global OECD survey.

---

23. http://www.oecd.org/site/netfwd

Figure 16: Evaluation of programs and foundations' performance

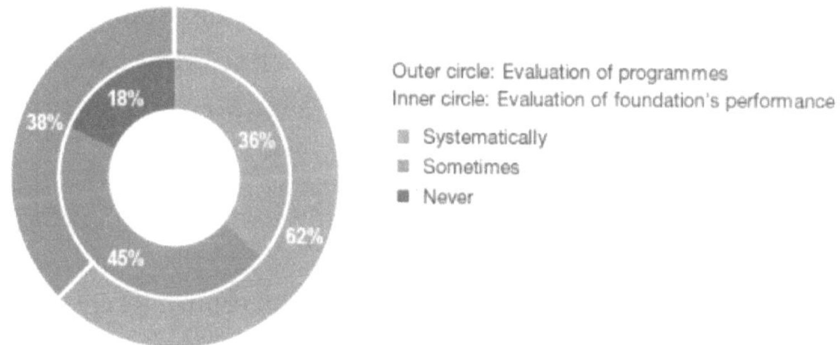

Source: OECD (2018), Survey on Private Philanthropy for Development 2013-15: Qualitative Questionnaire, www.oecd.org/site/netfwd[24].

Main private foundations and funders

Gates Foundation – Gender Equality Division[25]

The launch of the standalone Gender Equality Division within Gates Foundation in 2020 has furthered the foundation's commitment to gender equality outcomes across the United Nations Sustainable Development Goals. It builds on two decades of increasing investment in gender equality. The Gender Equality Division ensures that gender equality is incorporated across the foundation's work. Foundation's initiatives include women's economic empowerment, women's leadership, data and evidence, and innovation in science and technology to improve women's health. Foundation's focus is on reaching low-income women and girls in South Asia and sub-Saharan Africa, including Bangladesh, India, Ethiopia, Kenya, Nigeria, Tanzania, and Uganda.

Through the foundation's partners – from local nonprofits to in-country researchers, gender-focused coalitions, and governments –

---

24. http://www.oecd.org/site/netfwd

25. https://www.gatesfoundation.org/our-work/programs/gender-equality/gender-equality

they work to break down structural barriers to equality for women and girls and challenge the social norms that disadvantage them. Foundation also works to improve the lives of individual women by backing projects and programs that help them overcome day-to-day obstacles.

The Foundation for Gender Equality[26]

The Foundation for Gender Equality (FGE) dedicates to creating an urgent call to action on behalf of women and girls globally. Its strategic goals include developing new pathways to accelerate change, expanding opportunities and removing obstacles women and girls face around the world. Simply put, the FGE will help women and girls advance by fostering new collaborations and identifying practical, sustainable and successful programs that can be replicated. Furthermore, through its ongoing outreach, the FGE is committed to finding and supporting those precious grass-roots initiatives that are already making a difference for women and girls and, by extension, their families and communities.

Global Fund for Women[27]

Global Fund for Women is one of the world's leading organizations for gender equality and the human rights of girls and women. The organization was created to amplify the courageous work of women who are building social movements and challenging the *status quo*. This organization campaigns for zero violence, political and economic empowerment, sexual and reproductive health, and global women's rights.

The Global Fund for Women aims that every woman and girl realizes her fundamental rights for women's equality set out in the Universal

---

26. https://www.foundationforgenderequality.org/

27. https://www.globalfundforwomen.org/

Declaration of Human Rights. The Fund stands for a woman's right to decide when and if she wants to have a child and if so, to have high-quality health care during pregnancy and after birth. The Fund follows two critical documents about gender equality affecting women's rights in all aspects of life – the Convention on the Elimination of all Forms of Discrimination Against Women (CEDAW) and the Beijing Declaration and Platform for Action.

<u>MATCH International Women's Fund</u>[28]

MATCH International Women's Fund was established in 1976 to match the needs of Canadian women with the needs and resources of women around the world. MATCH International supports women innovators through their breakthroughs of transforming farming practices, child nutrition, and anti-violence campaigns. The Fund works with 650 women's organizations in 71 countries, and so far, it has invested nearly 12 million dollars in women and girls.

MATCH joined the women's fund movement and has officially launched the first Canada global fund for women, girls and transgender people in October 2013. Presently, the organization is the most direct way to get money into the hands of women's rights grassroots organizations. In this way, MATCH amplifies work on local levels and supports grassroots organizations breaking ground around the world. The goal and vision of the MATCH are to end violence and discrimination against women and girls.

<u>Equality fund</u>[29]

Powered by an initial CAD 300 million contributions from the Government of Canada, the Equality Fund is building the world's largest self-sustaining fund for gender equality. The fund offers a new

---

28. https://equalityfund.ca/

29. https://equalityfund.ca/

model for sustainable investment in gender equality everywhere. By transforming traditional approaches to development assistance, investing, and philanthropy simultaneously, the fund is trying to unlock capital to unleash the full power of women's movements worldwide. The fund participates in grantmaking, investment, advocacy, research, policymaking, etc.

Think tanks

Think tanks play an essential role in fostering more equitable and inclusive societies through their citizen and policy engagement. Their contributions to gender equality can be seen in their research and advocacy and making their organizations more gender-inclusive in policy and practice.

Gender equality is one of the critical areas of focus among many think tanks, including those receiving support from the Think Tank Initiative (TTI)[30]. The Think Tank Initiative (TTI) dedicates to strengthening the capacity of independent policy research institutions in the developing world. Launched in 2008 and managed by IDRC, TTI was a partnership between five donors. The program ended in 2019. This support allowed the institutions to attract, retain, and build local talent, develop an independent research program, and invest in public outreach to ensure that research results informed and influenced national and regional policy debates.

Almost all of the 50+ think tanks in the TTI initiative were engaged in gender-related work. They drew on TTI support to enhance their existing capacity to research and engage in gender theory, policy and practice and put gender at the core of their institutional sustainability plans.

---

30. https://www.idrc.ca/en/initiative/think-tank-initiative

The work of Grupo Sofia[31] exemplifies the role that think tanks can play in changing the perception of women in society. Four of Peru's leading social research institutions came together in 2014 to establish Grupo Sofia to address women's under-representation and lack of recognition in the social sciences. In addition, the group promotes the greater participation of women in academic publishing and knowledge sharing and in public debates and policy formulation.

In a series of studies on gender inequalities in the social sciences[32], Grupo Sofia found nearly twice as many men as women in higher academic posts and similar media and academic events disparities. In addition to raising awareness of these gaps, Grupo Sofia created practical tools to help universities and other organizations increase the participation of women. These included guidelines to ensure greater gender equality in research and policy events, which, in turn, influenced the event planning guidelines adopted for the final TTI Exchange. Grupo Sofia also published a directory of female social science experts for media and event organizers and studies of policy alternatives for tackling gender inequality in academia.

Other stakeholders

Networks and advocacy groups

Various networks, platforms for action, advocacy groups and initiatives at international, national and local levels grow in numbers and increasingly take more prominent roles. Through exchanges of ideas, resources and support, these initiatives are making significant advances

---

31. http://www.gruposofia.org.pe/

32. https://drive.google.com/file/d/

    0B4kljw8XggzpRDJaVnI3Sm15X0ZMNFE1anNGelBjZUE0WHVJ/

    view?resourcekey=0-7zx8HAQVntHj2kA2tSDvJw

in a broad scope of gender equality, including policy advocacy, human rights actions, data-gathering efforts, etc.

Rise Up[33]

Rise Up works on activating women and girls to transform their lives, families and communities through investing in local solutions, strengthening leadership, and building movements. The organisation's network of 500 leaders directly benefited around seven million girls and impacted around 100 laws and policies in Africa, Latin America, South Asia and the US.

Rise Up strengthens the leadership of women and girls to be able to drive changes in their communities. It focuses on advancing women's rights, equality, education, sexual and reproductive health, and economic empowerment. The organization conducts innovative programs and partners with both global and local organizations to achieve sustainable impact.

Gender at Work[34]

Gender at Work is an international feminist knowledge network working to build inclusive cultures and end discrimination against women. It partners up with researchers and activists worldwide to produce 1) new knowledge on inequality structures and embedded discriminatory societal norms and 2) innovative approaches and tools to transform them in organizations and communities.

The organization believes that the world is facing the crisis of democratic institutions: the actors who fight to achieve social justice have been undercut, and spaces for advocacy and action of civil society groups have been restricted. Therefore, Gender at Work offers a wide range of consulting services to organizations to strengthen their

33. https://riseuptogether.org/

34. https://genderatwork.org/

contributions to gender equality and advance feminist leadership. It also helps activists tell their stories and share their insights on gender inequalities with a broader public.

Men Engage Alliance[35]

Men Engage Alliance is a global alliance consisting of many country networks spread across many regions, hundreds of non-governmental organizations and UN agencies. It works towards advancing gender equality and justice, human rights and social justice, with a mission to achieve a world where all people can enjoy healthy and equitable relationships and their full potential.

The Men Engage Alliance works on engaging men and boys in gender equality and tries to build and improve men's engagement in achieving gender justice. It also advocates for policy changes on critical issues where gender directly affects the lives of women and men at local, national, regional and international levels. The organization works in the following areas: promoting sexual and reproductive health and rights, increasing HIV and AIDS prevention and treatment, ending violence against women and girls, combating homophobia/transphobia and advocating for LGBTI rights, reducing forms of violence between men and boys, preventing child sexual exploitation, sexual abuse and trafficking, supporting men's positive involvement in maternal and child health, as fathers or caregivers and addressing macro-level policies that perpetuate gender inequalities.

European Women's Lobby[36]

European Women's Lobby (EWL) is the largest European umbrella network of women's associations representing more than 2000 organizations in European Union Member States and candidate

---

35. http://menengage.org/

36. https://womenlobby.org/

countries. EWL envisions a society in which the contribution of women to all aspects of life is recognized and celebrated. That means that women should be recognised as leaders with self-confidence, freedom of choice and freedom from exploitation and violence.

EWL joins together the women's movement in Europe to support women's human rights and equality between women and men. Therefore, it offers its experiences, expertise and knowledge on gender equality and represents the women's voice in the EU political arenas. EWL also mobilizes its members' collective experiences to work on significant issues affecting women and connects different actors to bring change at the EU level.

Policy research institutes

International Center for Research on Women[37]

The International Center for Research on Women (ICRW) is a global research institute with headquarters in Washington D.C. and regional offices in India and Uganda. The ICRW comprises social scientists, economists, public health specialists, and demographers, all of whom are experts in gender issues. The guiding principle of ICRW's mission is human dignity, gender equity, inclusion and shared prosperity.

ICRW conducts research to tackle the causes of gender inequality and offers solutions for fundamental social change. The organization works with NGOs, government and private sector actors to conduct research and develop and guide strategies that build policies, programs and practices. In its research, ICRW identifies obstacles that prevent women from being economically empowered and fully participating in society. The ICRW translates these obstacles into a path of action that honours women's human rights and ensures gender equality.

---

37. https://www.icrw.org/

European Institute for Gender Equality[38]

The European Institute for Gender Equality (EIGE) was established in December 2006 as the European Union agency dedicated exclusively to gender equality. The task of the Institute is to collect and analyze information on gender equality to help the EU Member States implement gender equality policies and combat gender-based discrimination.

The Institute tackles both European and national policy areas by implementing the principle of gender mainstreaming to achieve equality of women and men in all spheres of life. The EIGE, thus, produces studies and collects statistics about gender equality in the EU and monitors how the EU meets the international standards about the issue. It also works to stop violence against women and shares its knowledge with other EU institutions.

Media

Media, both traditional and social, play an essential role in this field in informing the stakeholders about the new developments. Even more so, media set the topics and shape the worldviews affecting how its various stakeholders perceive gender equality issues. Unfortunately, media tend to perpetuate gender inequality. Research shows that gendered stereotypes presented in media influence children from a young age. Exposure to stereotypical gender portrayals and clear gender segregation is associated with 1) preferences for 'gender appropriate' media content, toys, games and activities, 2) traditional perceptions of gender roles, occupations and personality traits, and 3) certain expectations and aspirations for future trajectories of life. Women are frequently portrayed in stereotypical and hyper-sexualised roles in advertising and the film industry, with long-term social consequences.

---

38. https://eige.europa.eu/

Data shows that women only make up less than a quarter of the persons heard, read about or seen in newspaper, television and radio news. Even worse, almost half of news stories reinforce gender stereotypes, while only a few stories challenge gender stereotypes. And 73% of the media management jobs are occupied by men.

However, media can be part of the solution instead of being part of the problem. Indeed, it is hard to imagine achieving substantial improvements in gender equality worldwide without the transformative role that media needs to play. It can do so by creating gender-sensitive and gender-transformative content and breaking gender stereotypes. Media should also challenge traditional social and cultural norms and attitudes regarding gender perceptions in content and media houses' management. It can also help promote gender equality by showing women in leadership roles and as experts on various topics daily, not as an exception. The advent of the "Me Too" movement at social media in the US reverberated around the world over the past few years and has made a significant impact on the plethora of gender equality issues. It exemplifies the power of media in promoting gender equality and providing a transformative platform for fundamental social change.

4. Legal frameworks of gender equality

Over the last century, especially after the Second World War, a robust international framework for women's rights has developed. The international community has drafted several policy platforms and legal instruments to help countries worldwide achieve gender equality and women's empowerment. In the following paragraphs, We will outline some of the crucial developments and existing legal frameworks in this area.

1945: UN charter on human rights

The founding United Nations charter (1945) included a provision for equality between men and women (chapter III, article 8[1]). In particular, chapter III has an equal opportunity provision banning "restrictions on the eligibility of men and women to participate in any capacity and under conditions of equality in its principal and subsidiary organs."

1946: Commission on the Status of Women

The Commission on the Status of Women (CSW) is the principal global intergovernmental body exclusively dedicated to promoting gender equality and the empowerment of women. A functional commission of the Economic and Social Council (ECOSOC) was established in 1946. The CSW is instrumental in promoting women's rights, documenting the reality of women's lives throughout the world, and shaping global standards on gender equality and women's empowerment. The Commission's mandate expanded in 1996. It was decided that it should take a leading role in monitoring and reviewing

---

1. https://en.wikipedia.org/wiki/Chapter_III_of_the_United_Nations_Charter#Article_8

progress and problems in implementing the Beijing Declaration and Platform for Action (see below) and mainstreaming a gender perspective in UN activities. The Commission also contributes to the follow-up of the 2030 Agenda for Sustainable Development to accelerate gender equality and women's empowerment.

1979: Convention on the Elimination of All Forms of Discrimination Against Women

The **Convention on the Elimination of all Forms of Discrimination Against Women (CEDAW)** is an international treaty adopted in 1979 by the United Nations General Assembly. That is probably the single most crucial piece of legislation in the area of women's rights and gender equality globally. Described as an international bill of rights for women, the Convention was instituted on September 3, 1981, and ratified by 189 states. Over fifty countries that have ratified the Convention are subject to certain declarations, reservations, and objections, including 38 countries who rejected the enforcement article 29, which addresses means of settlement for disputes concerning the interpretation or application of the Convention. For example, Australia's declaration noted the limitations on central government power resulting from its federal constitutional system. Nevertheless, CEDAW is a global human rights treaty that should be incorporated into national law as the highest standard for women's rights. Moreover, it requires the UN Member States that have ratified it to set mechanisms to fully realise women's rights.

The Committee on the Elimination of Discrimination Against Women, usually abbreviated as 'CEDAW Committee', is the United Nations (UN) treaty body that oversees the Convention on the Elimination of All Forms of Discrimination Against Women (CEDAW) (UN CEDAW, 1989). The formation of this committee was outlined in Article 17 of the CEDAW, which also established the committee's rules, purpose, and operating procedures. The committee's task is to ensure that the regulations outlined in the CEDAW are being followed.

The CEDAW explicitly mandates signatory countries to enshrine gender equality into their domestic legislation, repeal all discriminatory provisions in their laws, and enact new provisions to guard against discrimination against women. Signatory countries must also establish tribunals and public institutions to guarantee women's adequate protection against discrimination and take steps to eliminate all forms of discrimination practised against women by individuals, organisations, and enterprises. The CEDAW also requires signatory countries to guarantee basic human rights and fundamental freedoms to women "on the basis of equality with men" through the "political, social, economic, and cultural fields." It further notes that "adoption... of special measures aimed at accelerating *de facto* equality between men and women shall not be considered discrimination." It also adds that special protection for maternity is not regarded as gender discrimination. Notably, the Convention also requires signatory countries to eliminate prejudices and customs based on the idea of the inferiority or the superiority of one sex or the stereotyped role for men and women. It also mandates the states parties "[t]o ensure... the recognition of the common responsibility of men and women in the upbringing and development of their children." The Convention also mandates the state parties for relevant actions to ensure gender equality in the following areas: participation in governmental bodies, nationality laws, education, right to work, equal pay, social benefits, healthcare, family planning, economic and social life, representation before the law, movement of people, marriage provisions, etc. Notably, the convention also obliges states parties to "take all appropriate measures, including legislation, to suppress all forms of trafficking in women and exploitation of the prostitution of women. In addition, it guarantees women's equality in political and public life, focusing on equality in voting, participation in government, participation in "non-governmental organisations and associations concerned with the public and political life of the country." (Full set of CEDAW's Core Provisions is available in **Appendix 1**.

1993: The Vienna Declaration and Programme of Action (VDPA)

The Vienna Declaration and Programme of Action (VDPA) is a human rights declaration adopted by consensus at the World Conference on Human Rights[2] on June 25, 1993, in Vienna, Austria. This declaration recognises women's rights as being protected human rights. Paragraph 18 reads: "The human rights of women and of the girl-child are an inalienable, integral and indivisible part of universal human rights. The full and equal participation of women in political, civil, economic, social and cultural life, at the national, regional and international levels, and the eradication of all forms of discrimination on the grounds of sex are priority objectives of the international community." VDPA also explicitly recognises gender-based violence, sexual harassment and exploitation.

The VDPA concludes by proclaiming women's rights and gender-based exploitation as legitimate issues for the international community. That was a critical point of consensus that has led to the establishment of several international inter-governmental organisations on women's rights and gender equality and their incorporation in the work programs of numerous existing international organisations.

1995: World Conference on Women – Beijing Platform for Action

The **Fourth World Conference on Women: Action for Equality, Development and Peace** was the name for a conference convened by

---

2. https://en.wikipedia.org/wiki/World_Conference_on_Human_Rights

the United Nations during September 4-15, 1995, in Beijing, China. At this conference, governments worldwide agreed on a comprehensive plan to achieve global legal equality, known as the Beijing Platform for Action (UN, 1995).

The Platform for Action is an agenda for women's empowerment. The Platform for Action reaffirms the fundamental principle outlined in the Vienna Declaration and Programme of Action, that the human rights of women and of the girl child are an inalienable, integral and indivisible part of universal human rights. As an agenda for action, the Platform seeks to promote and protect the full enjoyment of all human rights and the fundamental freedoms of all women throughout their life cycle.

The Platform lists several 'critical areas of concern'. It outlines the existing problem and proposes strategic objectives with concrete actions to be taken by various actors to achieve those objectives (see **Appendix 2** for a complete list of these strategic objectives).

The Beijing Platform for Action played an important role in invigorating the international community in the area of women's rights and gender equality, stimulating further institutional strengthening at both international and national levels. The Beijing Platform for Action still represents one of the cornerstones of international women's rights frameworks, with the UN Women launching Beijing 20+ (in 2014) and Beijing 25+ (in 2019) initiatives, referring to the landmark conference in 1995 in Beijing.

2010: UN Women

In 2010, the United Nations General Assembly voted unanimously to create a new entity to accelerate progress in meeting the needs of women and girls worldwide. The UN Entity for Gender Equality and the Empowerment of Women[3] - known as "UN Women" — is a result of years of negotiations between the UN Member States and advocacy by the global women's movement. The creation of UN Women came about as part of the UN reform agenda, bringing together resources and mandates for greater impact. It merges and builds on the important work of four previously distinct parts of the UN system, which focused exclusively on gender equality and women's empowerment.

UN Women was given two key roles: It is tasked with supporting inter-governmental bodies such as the Commission on the Status of Women in their formulation of policies, global standards and norms, and it will help the Member States to implement these standards, standing ready to provide suitable technical and financial support to those countries that request it, as well as forging effective partnerships with civil society. It will also help the UN system to be accountable for its own commitments on gender equality, including regular monitoring of system-wide progress.

UN Women is the United Nations entity dedicated to gender equality and the empowerment of women. A global champion for women and girls, UN Women was established to accelerate progress on meeting their needs worldwide. UN Women supports UN Member States as they set global standards for achieving gender equality, and works with governments and civil society to design laws, policies, programmes and services needed to ensure that the standards are effectively implemented and truly benefit women and girls worldwide. It works globally to make the vision of the Sustainable Development Goals a reality for women and girls and stands behind women's equal participation in all aspects of life.

---

3. https://www.unwomen.org/en

2017: Sustainable Development Goals[4] (SDGs)

The **Sustainable Development Goals (SDGs)** or **Global Goals** are a collection of 17 interlinked global goals designed to be a "blueprint for achieving a better and more sustainable future for all". The SDGs were set up in 2015 by the United Nations General Assembly and intended to be achieved by 2030 (UN, 2017).

Sustainable Development Goal 5 (SDG 5 or Global Goal 5) reads: "Achieve gender equality and empower all women and girls". Determined indicators measure progress towards goals and targets. The 17 SDGs recognise that action in one area will affect outcomes in others and that development must balance social, economic and environmental sustainability. We will discuss SDGs and related issues in more detail in the following sections.

Related international legislation

Apart from the legislation primarily focused on gender equality and women's rights, other international legal frameworks were developed over time, addressing some aspects of these issues. For example, in 2000, the United Nations Security Council unanimously adopted the United Nations Security Council Resolution requiring all states to respect fully international humanitarian law and international human rights law applicable to the rights and protection of women and girls during and after the armed conflicts.

Regional legislation

On top of the legal frameworks developed to be applied globally, numerous regional frameworks simultaneously emerged worldwide. For example, the Maputo Protocol[5] adopted by the African Union in

---

4. https://www.un.org/sustainabledevelopment/sustainable-development-goals/

5. https://en.wikipedia.org/wiki/Maputo_Protocol

the form of a protocol to the African Charter on Human and People's Rights in 2005 guarantees comprehensive rights to women, including the right to take part in the political process, to social and political equality with men, to control their reproductive health, and to end female genital mutilation.

Likewise, the European Union's Directive in 2002 states that: "Harassment and sexual harassment within the meaning of this Directive shall be deemed to be discrimination on the grounds of sex and therefore prohibited." Furthermore, the Council of Europe has developed *Gender Equality Strategy 2014–2017*, which has five strategic objectives:

- Combating gender stereotypes[6] and sexism
- Preventing and combating violence against women[7]
- Guaranteeing Equal Access of Women to Justice
- Achieving balanced participation of women and men in political and public decision-making
- Achieving Gender Mainstreaming[8] in all policies and measures

On top of these international frameworks, each country has its own legislative and institutional framework that regulates various aspects of gender equality.

---

6. https://en.wikipedia.org/wiki/Gender_stereotypes

7. https://en.wikipedia.org/wiki/Violence_against_women

8. https://en.wikipedia.org/wiki/Gender_mainstreaming

5. Dimensions of gender equality used in the international empirical research

Whether it is a predominantly legal, empirical or political framework, gender equality is always a multidimensional construct. These aspects and dimensions vary across frameworks regarding their number, granularity and content. Yet, similarities and overlaps do exist along with unique focuses of some of the frameworks to less noticed aspects. In the following paragraphs, we will present dimensions of gender equality as outlined in some of the key institutions.

UN – Sustainable Development Goals

SDG 5 on gender equality has nine targets and 17 indicators. Six of the targets are "outcome-oriented":

1. ending all forms of discrimination against all women and girls everywhere;
2. ending violence and exploitation of women and girls;
3. eliminating harmful practices such as child, early and forced marriage and female genital mutilation;
4. increasing value of unpaid care and promoting shared domestic responsibilities;
5. ensuring full participation of women in leadership and decision-making; and
6. ensuring access to universal reproductive rights and health.

The three "means of achieving" targets are:

1. fostering equal rights to economic resources, property

       ownership and financial services for women;

2. promoting the empowerment of women through technology; and

3. adopting, strengthening policies and enforcing legislation for gender equality.

However, it is essential to note that the issue of gender equality in the SDGs framework is not related only to the fulfilment of these nine targets and their 17 indicators. There is, in fact, a much larger number of gender-specific indicators among all SDGs, as discussed in more detail in the following section.

The United Nations Minimum Set of Gender Indicators

A product of the Inter-agency and Expert Group on Gender Statistics (see below) and agreed by the United Nations Statistical Commission in 2013, the Minimum Set of Gender Indicators is designed to be used across countries and regions for the national production and international compilation of gender statistics.

The indicators are organised into five domains:

- Economic structures and access to resources,
- Education,
- Health and related services,
- Public life and decision-making, and
- Human rights of women and children.

Each domain addresses one or more of the Beijing Platform for Action critical areas of concern. However, due to either data's unavailability or vague concepts and definitions, three of the 12 crucial areas of concern are not covered in the minimal set of gender indicators.

The IAEG-GS updated the Minimum Set of Gender Indicators over the years. The latest update in 2019[1] took into account updated tier classification for SDG indicators and resulted in 52 quantitative and 11 qualitative indicators (UN DESA, 2019). Among the quantitative indicators, there are 34 Tier 1 indicators, 13 Tier 2 indicators, 4 Tier 3 indicators, and 1 indicator classified as both Tier 1 and Tier 2. Among the qualitative indicators, there are 10 Tier 1 indicators and 1 Tier 2 indicator.

European Union – Gender Equality (European Institute for Gender Equality - EIGE)

EIGE is European Union's research institute explicitly established for research on gender equality and related topics. As one of its main products, the institute has developed the Gender Equality Index as "a tool to measure the progress of gender equality in the EU, developed by EIGE. It gives more visibility to areas that need improvement and ultimately supports policymakers to design more effective gender equality measures."

The Index includes information from six "key domains": work, money, knowledge, time, power & health with two "additional domains": violence against women and intersecting inequalities. Each domain has a set of subdomains/indicators – 31 in total – assessed and used in the overall evaluation and index creation.

The Index also examines how elements such as disability, age, level of education, country of birth and family type intersect with gender to create different pathways in people's lives.

---

1. https://genderstats.un.org/files/Minimum%20Set%20indicators%202018.11.1%20web.pdf

Beijing Platform for Action (UN lead)

The Beijing Declaration and Platform for Action is widely known as the most progressive blueprint for advancing women's rights (UN, 1995). The framework covers 12 areas of concern (complete list of domains and subdomains available in **Appendix 2**):

1. Women and the environment
2. Women in power and decision making
3. The girl child
4. Women and the economy
5. Women and poverty
6. Violence against women
7. Human rights of women
8. Education and training of women
9. Institutional mechanisms for the advancement of women
10. Women and health
11. Women and the media
12. Women and armed conflict

UN Women:

All human development and human rights issues have gender dimensions. UN Women focuses on priority areas that are fundamental to women's equality and unlock progress across the board. These include:

1. Leadership and political participation[2]
2. Economic empowerment[3]
3. Ending violence against women[4]

---

2. https://www.unwomen.org/en/what-we-do/leadership-and-political-participation

3. https://www.unwomen.org/en/what-we-do/economic-empowerment

4. https://www.unwomen.org/en/what-we-do/ending-violence-against-women

4. Peace and security[5]
5. Humanitarian action[6]
6. Governance and national planning[7]
7. Youth[8]
8. Women and girls with disabilities[9]
9. SDGs (all 17 criteria)
10. HIV and AIDS[10]

World Bank

World Development Report (2016) of the World Bank identified three critical domains of gender inequality: endowment, economic opportunity and agency (World Bank, 2016). For each dimension or broad area, it highlights the main incorporated issues. For example, the area of endowment comprises gender gaps in education and increased female mortality at specific life cycle periods (at birth, in infancy and reproductive years). In the area of economic opportunities, it discusses excessive time spent by women on domestic work and childcare, the gender gaps in access to assets and inputs, and the continuing discrimination in paid employment. Regarding the agency, the key issue continues to be women's lack of societal voice due to underrepresentation in national and local decision-making bodies, the weakness of women's voices within the household, and their exposure to gender-based violence.

The World Bank's conceptual framework on gender equality (**Figure 17**) emphasises the multi-causal nature of the construct and this

---

5. https://www.unwomen.org/en/what-we-do/peace-and-security

6. https://www.unwomen.org/en/what-we-do/humanitarian-action

7. https://www.unwomen.org/en/what-we-do/governance-and-national-planning

8. https://www.unwomen.org/en/what-we-do/youth

9. https://www.unwomen.org/en/what-we-do/women-and-girls-with-disabilities

10. https://www.unwomen.org/en/what-we-do/hiv-and-aids

phenomenon. It states that households, markets, institutions (both formal and informal) and their interactions all affect gender equality. Households are composed of individuals with varying preferences and needs, thus creating heterogeneous units. Markets and institutions influence the relationship between gender equality and economic development both directly and indirectly. They are also dynamic systems, under continuous societal influence, including policy interventions. Thus, how household members make decisions, how they interact with institutions and markets, and how the policy influences these interactions all shape gender equality outcomes in a given society (World Bank, 2011).

Figure 17: Conceptual framework of the World Bank on Gender Equality

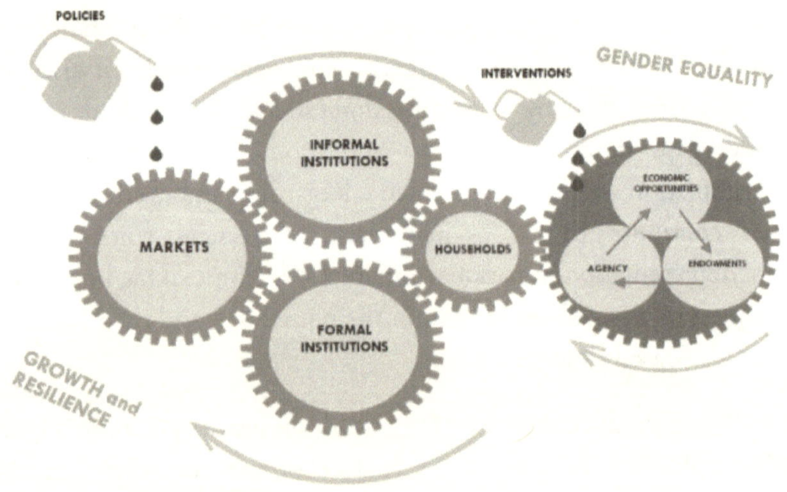

Source: Adapted from the 2012 World Development Report (World Bank, 2011)

World Economic Forum

The World Economic Forum's flagship Global Gender Gap Index is calculated across four key dimensions (sub-indices) and 14 indicators, as follows:

- Economic Participation and Opportunity
    - Labour force participation rate (%)
    - Wage equality for similar work (survey, 1–7 scale)
    - Estimated earned income (PPP, int.$)
    - Legislators, senior officials and managers (%)
    - Professional and technical workers (%)
- Educational Attainment
    - Literacy rate (%)
    - Enrolment in primary education (%)
    - Enrolment in secondary education (%)
    - Enrolment in tertiary education (%)
- Health and Survival and
    - Sex ratio at birth (%)
    - Healthy life expectancy (years)
- Political Empowerment
    - Women in parliament (%)
    - Women in ministerial positions (%)
    - Years with female head of state (last 50), the share of tenure years

Indicators within each of the four sub-indices are averaged, and the four sub-indices are calculated for each participating country. After that, overall index scores of gender gaps are calculated with equal participation/weight of all four dimensions/sub-indices.

United Nation Economic Commission for Europe (UNECE)

The 2010 UNECE Work Session on Gender Statistics established a task force to review the existing indicators across various frameworks and produce a new set of indicators that would allow for detailed monitoring of internationally agreed policy agendas.

The UNECE Task Force started its work in 2010 and systematically reviewed existing frameworks and statistics available. Conceptually, the Beijing Platform for Action (BPA) (United Nations, 1995) is a starting point for identifying the domains of gender equality because it provides an internationally agreed framework for establishing a relationship between the indicators and the policy concerns.

In the resulting UNECE framework[11] (UNECE, 2015), indicators are proposed in the following domains:

- Poverty
- Education and training
- Health
- Violence against women
- Economy, including the labour market and work-and-family issues
- Women in power and decision-making
- Media
- Environment
- The girl child

Summary

There is substantial similarity across conceptualisations of different aspects or dimensions of gender equality across various frameworks

---

11. https://unece.org/DAM/stats/publications/2015/ECE_CES_37_WEB.pdf

and institutions. Yet, apparent differences often reflect the particular institutional background, focus or scope, and other factors.

Summarising existing listings of dimensions of gender equality, we could broadly (and arguably) divide them into the three tentative groups, based on how frequently they are included in various frameworks:

The most commonly mentioned:

- Economic conditions
- Health
- Education
- Political participation

Often mentioned:

- Violence against women
- Work vs money vs wealth/ownership (disaggregated economic indicators)
- Access to political vs economic power vs equal treatment by a government (disaggregated political indicators)
- Legal framework (enshrined gender equality)

Rarely mentioned:

- Intersecting inequalities
- Social norms and values
- Media
- Environment
- Deeper power structures and inequalities (feminism, critical theory, etc.)

We should also note that most frameworks indicate the inter-dependability of various dimensions and their interaction with other related aspects. Thus, it should be taken as common knowledge that the situation and gender parity in one specified area are not independent of the situation in other outlined areas. Furthermore, some frameworks distinguish between 1) some dimensions and indicators that could be seen as outcomes or goals and 2) others that are conceptually seen as necessary tools for achieving gender equality. Finally, most of the frameworks also offer a hierarchical structure of the outlined dimensions, often consisting of three layers – two conceptual layers and a layer of empirical indicators:

- Broad dimensions

- Narrower aspects of dimensions

- Empirical measures of more limited aspects

Conceptual structures offered by legal frameworks (e.g. Beijing Platform for Action) differ from those developed by empirically-driven frameworks (e.g. WEF's Global Gender Gap Index). Empirically-driven frameworks (WEF's, World Bank's, OECD's, EIGE's, etc.) are much more aligned with one another and primarily focus on capturing quantitative indicators that have available data in most countries globally. On the other hand, legally-driven frameworks predominantly focus on human rights, institutional issues, and qualitative indicators.

6. Empirical evidence on gender equality across identified dimensions

Many governmental, non-governmental, academic organisations and coalitions are actively involved in empirical research on gender equality (see **Figure 18**), either as their primary subject or as one of their topics of interest. This section will outline only the main lines of work of some of the key players and contributors in this area.

International intergovernmental organisations

UN – Sustainable Development Goals:

The 2030 Agenda for Sustainable Development is a landmark agreement negotiated and signed by the 193 Member States of the United Nations (UN, 2017). Comprised of 17 Sustainable Development Goals (SDGs), 169 targets, and 232 indicators, it addresses sustainable development's economic, social, and environmental dimensions. The SDGs global indicator framework is far more ambitious and comprehensive than its predecessor, the Millennium Development Goals (MDGs) framework (UN, 2015a). It includes 54 gender-specific indicators integrated across different goals and covers areas new to global monitoring efforts, such as unpaid care, domestic work and violence against women and girls. That means that the indicator framework is gender-sensitive in 6 out of 17 goals, gender-sparse in 5 domains and gender-blind in the remaining six areas.

Figure 18: 54 Gender-specific Indicators of the SDGs

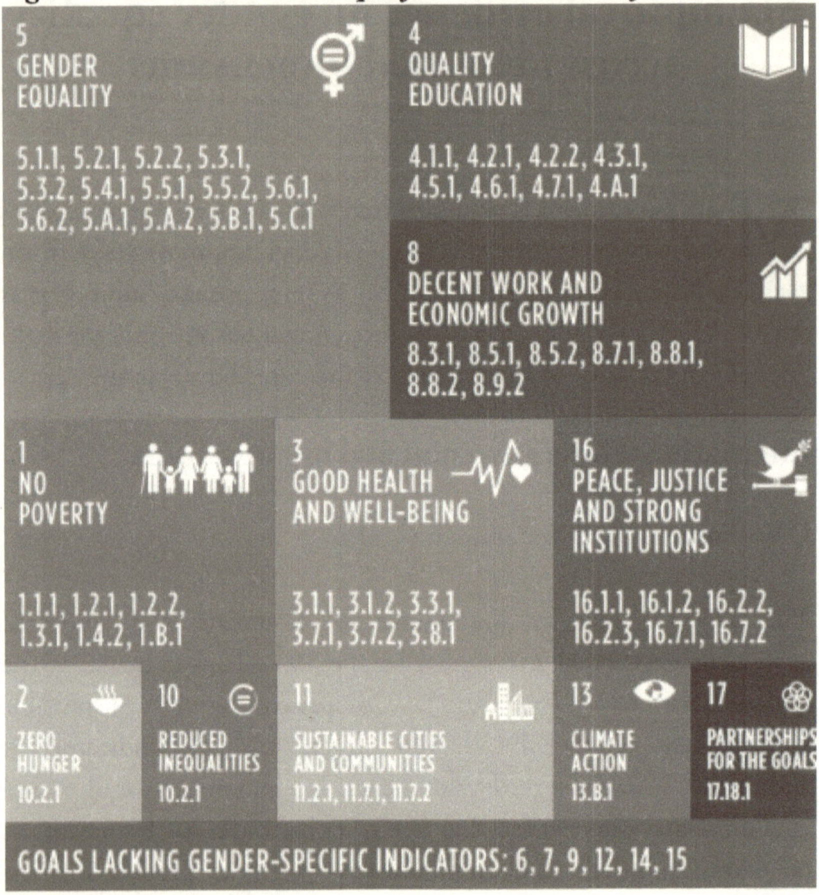

Source: UN Women, 2018.

In 2015, the United Nations Statistical Commission created the Inter-agency and Expert Group on SDG Indicators[1] (IAEG-SDGs), composed of Member States and including regional and international agencies as observers. The IAEG-SDGs had a task to develop and implement the global indicator framework for the Goals and targets of the 2030 Agenda. As a result, the global indicator framework was developed by the IAEG-SDGs and agreed upon, including refinements

---

1. https://unstats.un.org/sdgs/iaeg-sdgs/

and regular updates introduced during later sessions. The current status of the SDG indicators, including those from the SDG 5 on Gender Equality, regarding their classification into the tiers and assigned custodian agencies for providing related empirical data, is available in the attached Excel file.

World Economic Forum (The Global Gender Gap)

The World Economic Forum – particularly its Centre for the New Economy and Society[2] – researches gender gaps with a growing portfolio of initiatives. Among these, the Global Gender Gap Index[3] is its flagship program to benchmark the evolution of gender-based gaps and tracks progress towards closing these gaps over time.

In its 2021 round[4], the Global Gender Gap Index benchmarked 156 countries, providing a cross-country comparison tool and prioritising the most effective policies needed to close gender gaps (World Economic Forum, 2021). The methodology of the index has remained stable since its original conception in 2006, providing a basis for robust cross-country and time-series analysis. The Global Gender Gap Index measures scores on a 0 to 100 scale, which can be interpreted as the distance to parity (i.e. the percentage of the gender gap that has been closed).

The Global Gender Statistics Programme & the Inter-Agency and Expert Group on Gender Statistics IAEG-GS

The Global Gender Statistics Programme is mandated by the United Nations Statistical Commission, implemented by the United Nations

---

2. https://www.weforum.org/platforms/shaping-the-future-of-the-new-economy-and-society

3. https://www.weforum.org/reports/ab6795a1-960c-42b2-b3d5-587eccda6023

4. https://www3.weforum.org/docs/WEF_GGGR_2021.pdf

Statistics Division (UNSD) and coordinated by the Inter-Agency and Expert Group on Gender Statistics IAEG-GS.

The Programme is tasked with:

- improving coherence among existing initiatives on gender statistics through international coordination
- developing and promoting methodological guidelines in existing domains as well as in emerging areas of gender concern
- strengthening national statistical and technical capacity for the production, dissemination and use of gender-relevant data
- facilitating access to gender-relevant data and metadata through a newly developed data portal (forthcoming).

The IAEG-GS brings together representatives of international agencies within and outside the United Nations system, statisticians from National Statistical Systems, and development partners to review progress and guide future activities geared at advancing gender statistics. The UN Statistics Division is the secretariat of the group.

United Nations Statistics Division (UNSD) serves as Secretariat of the Inter-Agency and Expert Group on Gender Statistics (IAEG-GS), the coordinating and guiding body of the Global Gender Statistics Programme. The IAEG-GS was first convened in 2006, meets annually and functions through advisory groups. Presently, the leading advisory group's work examines emerging and unaddressed key gender issues and related data gaps to develop proposals to fill these gaps. The results of the IAEG-GS and the UNSD under the Global Gender Statistics Programme are presented to the United Nation's Economic and Social Council in yearly reports (available here[5]).

---

5. https://unstats.un.org/unsd/demographic-social/gender/

UN Women

UN Women is one of the most important international organisations in the area of gender equality. It organises many initiatives across various UN institutions and leads global policy and empirical activities in this area.

Women Count

Among its most important contributions in the empirical aspect of its work is its establishment of the Women Count hub[6] that offers easily accessible gender equality data in one place. For example, on the Women Count platform, one can find updated data on gender-specific SDG indicators and data for UN Women's flagship report Progress of the World's Women, along with data on women, peace and security, and violence against women.

Progress on the Sustainable Development Goals: The Gender Snapshot

The 2021 edition of Progress on the Sustainable Development Goals: The Gender Snapshot 2021[7] brings together the latest available evidence on gender equality across all 17 Sustainable Development Goals (UN Women, 2021). It highlights the progress made since 2015, but also the continued alarm over the COVID-19 pandemic and its immediate effect on women's well-being, including the threat it poses to future generations (**Figure 19**).

Figure 19: Except from the 2021 Progress on the SDG. The Gender Snapshot

---

6. https://data.unwomen.org/publications/women-count-annual-report-2020

7. https://data.unwomen.org/publications/progress-sustainable-development-goals-gender-snapshot-2021

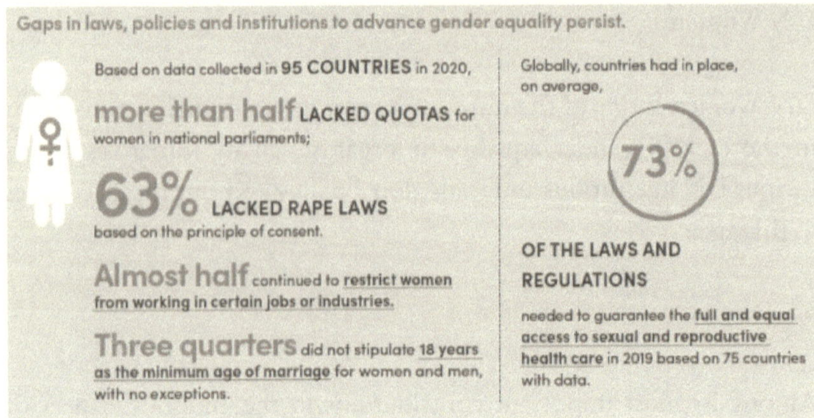

Source: *UN Women, 2021.*

World survey on the role of women in development

The "World survey on the role of women in development[8]" comes out every five years and is focused on selected emerging development themes that impact the role of women in the economy at the national, regional, and international levels. The "World survey" brings a gender perspective into economic and development issues. The latest (eighth) "World survey" (2019) focuses on the reasons for the high levels of income poverty and time poverty among women. It contains the rationale for taking an integrated policy approach to addressing the double bind experienced by women in that regard, as a timely and relevant means of achieving sustainable development, particularly in low-income contexts.

World Bank, World Development Indicators data portal

The World Bank is one of the most important and most active global institutions in the area of gender equality policy research and

---

8. https://www.unwomen.org/en/digital-library/world-survey-on-the-role-of-women-in-development

interventions. In its recently published Gender Equality Strategy[9] (World Bank, 2015), developed through consultations with more than 1,000 stakeholders from 22 countries and diverse backgrounds, it reflects on changes in the global landscape and the accumulation of evidence about what works to close gaps. The Strategy recognises that more vigorous and better-resourced efforts are needed to address gender inequalities in access to jobs and control over and ownership of productive assets. The Strategy presents the World Bank's conceptual framework on gender equality (**Figure 17**) and the overview of empirical evidence and its gaps.

The World Bank also regularly tracks gender equality statistics and publishes its findings. One of the leading publications in this area is World Bank's Little Data Book on Gender. The Little Data Book on Gender 2019[10] illustrates the progress towards gender equality for 217 economies worldwide (World Bank, 2019). It provides comparable statistics for women and men for 2000 and 2017 across various indicators covering education, health and related services, economic structure, participation and access to resources, public life, decision making, and agency, enabling readers to compare economies.

The World Bank also organises the Umbrella Facility for Gender Equality[11] (UFGE), a multi-donor trust fund financing research, impact evaluations and data to help policymakers and practitioners close gender gaps in countries and sectors. The UFGE has financed work in over 90 countries, influencing policies and programs and changing how companies work.

---

9. https://openknowledge.worldbank.org/handle/10986/23425

10. https://openknowledge.worldbank.org/handle/10986/31689

11. https://www.worldbank.org/en/programs/umbrellafacilityforgenderequality

UNESCO, Institute for Statistics

The UNESCO Institu te for Statistics (UIS) is the official source of internationally comparable data on education, science, culture and communication. To help countries fulfil their promise to close the gender gap[12] by 2030, the UIS disaggregates all indicators by sex to the extent possible, produces parity indices and develops new indicators to reflect the equity and inclusion of girls and boys. For example, UIS data allow us to see and compare the extent to which girls start primary school, such as repeat grades, drop out, or transition to secondary education. In addition, the UIS is developing new global measures of learning outcomes[13] to better evaluate girls' and boys' reading and numeracy skills at critical points in their education.

UIS has recently also launched eAtlas of Gender Inequality in Education[14] to track progress and pitfalls in countries worldwide. A series of interactive maps and charts bring to life an extraordinary range of data for about 200 countries produced by the UIS, the official data source for the global goal of education.

United Nation Statistics Directorate (UNSD)

Statistics Division of the United Nations Department of Economic and Social Affairs produces the World's Women report[15] every five years since 1990. It provides the latest data on the state of gender equality worldwide. The report compiles 100 data stories that give a snapshot of the state of gender equality worldwide. Presented on an interactive portal, the report analyses gender equality in six critical areas: population and families; health; education; economic

---

12. http://uis.unesco.org/en/topic/equity-education

13. http://uis.unesco.org/en/topic/learning-outcomes

14. http://uis.unesco.org/en/news/uis-launches-eatlas-gender-inequality-education

15. http://unstats.un.org/unsd/demographic-social/products/worldswomen/

empowerment and asset ownership; power and decision-making; and violence against women and the girl child, as well as the impact of COVID-19. The vast database on which the report is based is available for in-depth exploration and analysis.

UNSD also provides the most comprehensive, broad, up-to-date and relevant global database for measuring and monitoring the UN's SDGs, including those in the SDG 5 domain on gender equality. Global Database gives access to data on more than 210 SDG for countries across the globe by indicator, country, region or period. The database is available here[16].

OECD

The Organisation for Economic Cooperation and Development (OECD) is another prominent and influential global institution that dedicates a substantial part of its resources and activities to gender equality issues. OECD's Gender Initiative[17] examines existing barriers to gender equality in education, employment, and entrepreneurship. It monitors the progress made by governments to promote gender equality in both OECD and non-OECD countries and provides good practices based on analytical tools and reliable data.

Gender Data Portal

The OECD's Gender Data Portal[18] includes about 75 indicators shedding light on gender inequalities in education, employment, entrepreneurship, health, development and governance, showing how far we are from achieving gender equality and where actions are most

---

16. https://unstats.un.org/sdgs/UNSDG/IndDatabasePage

17. https://www.oecd.org/gender/

18. https://www.oecd.org/gender/data/

needed. The data cover OECD member countries and partner economies, including Brazil, China, India, Indonesia, and South Africa. The portal classifies gender equality data across six domains:

- Employment
- Education
- Entrepreneurship
- Health
- Development
- Governance

OECD provides gender equality data through its gender-specific indicators in its data repositories on employment, entrepreneurship, education, family, development, health, etc. (complete list available here[19]). In addition, OECD runs several global survey programmes, such as PISA, PIAAC, SSES, etc., that are collecting internationally comparable data on various topics, most of which are also gender-specific.

The Gender, Institutions and Development Database

The GID-DB[20] database provides researchers and policymakers with essential data on gender-based discrimination in social institutions. This data helps analyse women's economic empowerment and understand gender gaps in other critical areas of development. Covering 180 countries and territories, the GID-DB contains a comprehensive view of legal, cultural and traditional practices that discriminate against women and girls.

---

19. https://www.oecd.org/gender/resources/

20. https://stats.oecd.org/index.aspx?datasetcode=GIDDB2014

Social Institutions and Gender Index (SIGI)

The OECD Development Centre's Social Institutions and Gender Index[21] (SIGI) measures discrimination against women in social institutions across 180 countries. By taking into account laws, social norms and practices, the SIGI captures the underlying drivers of gender inequality, intending to provide the data necessary for transformative policy change. The SIGI is also one of the official data sources for monitoring SDG 5.1.1 "Whether or not legal frameworks are in place to promote, enforce and monitor gender equality and women's empowerment." The index provides measures across four domains (**Figure 20**).

Figure 20: The composition of the SIGI 2019

---

21. https://www.genderindex.org/

Source: OECD, 2019a.

United Nations Development Program (UNDP)

UNDP is another UN institution that deals with gender equality issues. Its flagship program in this area is Gender Inequality Index (GII). The GII measures gender inequalities in three critical aspects of human development:

1. reproductive health, measured by maternal mortality ratio and adolescent birth rates;
2. empowerment, measured by the proportion of parliamentary seats occupied by females and proportion of adult females and males aged 25 years and older with at least some secondary

education; and

3. economic status expressed as labour market participation and measured by labour force participation rate of female and male populations aged 15 years and older.

The GII is built on the same framework as the UNDP's International Human Development Index – to expose differences in the distribution of achievements between women and men. It measures the human development costs of gender inequality in 162 countries. Thus, the higher the GII value, the more disparities between females and males and the more considerable loss to human development.

The GII sheds new light on the position of women in 162 countries; it yields insights into gender gaps in major areas of human development. The component indicators highlight areas in need of critical policy intervention, and it stimulates proactive thinking and public policy to overcome systematic disadvantages of women (**Figure 21**).

Figure 21: The structure of the Gender Inequality Index

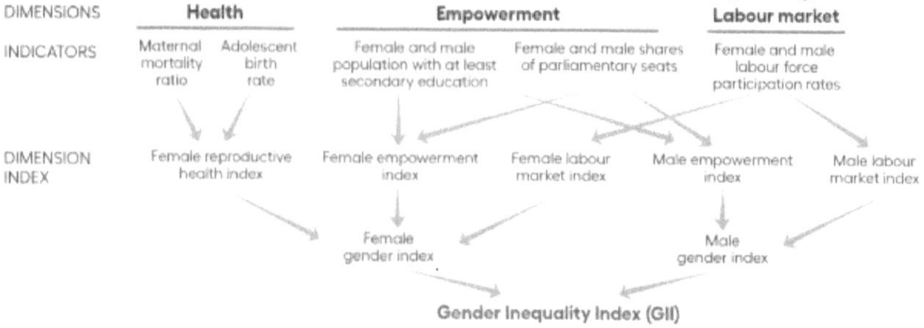

Source: UNPD, 2020.

The Gender Development Index (GDI) measures gender inequalities in achievement in three basic dimensions of human development: health, measured by female and male life expectancy at birth; education, measured by female and male expected years of schooling for children and female and male mean years of schooling for adults ages 25 years and older; and command over economic resources, measured by female and male estimated earned income (**Figure 22**).

Figure 22: The structure of the Gender Development Index

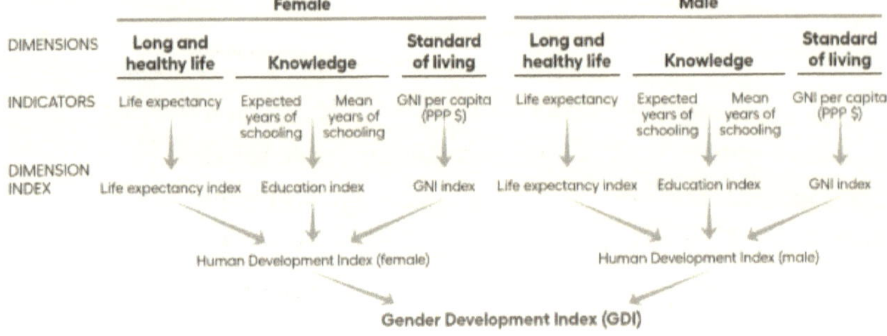

Source: UNPD, 2020.

The UNDP also offers a vast database, Human Development Data Center[22], with a comprehensive depository of gender-specific data, at national, regional and international levels.

UNICEF

UNICEF is another UN organisation that conducts important empirical work in the area of gender equality, in particular concerning children and adolescents around the world. To monitor the status of women and children and track progress toward the 2030 Agenda for Sustainable Development's commitment to gender equality, UNICEF produces, compiles, analyses and disseminates gender statistics across a wide range of sectors, including education, health, protection from violence and exploitation, and water, sanitation and hygiene (WASH). It does this by:

- Ensuring that the data collection process does not introduce gender bias and yields high-quality gender data.

---

22. http://hdr.undp.org/en/data

- Maintaining global databases[23] sourced from administrative records, vital registrations, population censuses and household surveys on various sex-disaggregated and gender-specific indicators to build the evidence base on gender equality and the rights and well-being of children.
- Cross-disaggregating gender- and child-related indicators by sex and key stratifiers, including wealth, location and age, to better understand which women, girls, and boys are most marginalised.
- Improving the use of gender statistics through better dissemination and communication channels and developing innovative methodologies for filling gender data gaps.

Another vital contribution of UNICEF to gender equality research is its Multiple Indicator Cluster Survey (MICS)[24]. This survey is UNICEF's main instrument to gather nationally representative sex-disaggregated and gender-relevant data for children, women and men. Access a list of sex-disaggregated and gender-specific indicators available in MICS[25].

Other international organisations

Many other international institutions conduct research, provide empirical data and publish results and policy reports in some of the domains of gender equality. We will list some of these, many of which belong to the United Nation's system and many others who are relevant international or regional stakeholders in this field. These include:

- International Labour Organisation[26]

---

23. https://data.unicef.org/topic/gender/overview/

24. https://mics.unicef.org/

25. https://data.unicef.org/wp-content/uploads/2021/09/MICS6-Gender-Indicators.pdf

- United Nations Population Fund (UNFPA), State of World Population 2020[27]
- UNODC - United Nations Office on Drugs and Crime[28]
- FAO - The Food and Agriculture Organization of the UN[29]
- International Telecommunication Union (ILU)[30]
- EU Database on gender balance in decision-making positions[31]
- GEM: Global Entrepreneurship Monitor[32]
- Women in national parliaments[33]

Private-public partnerships and civic initiatives

Apart from the inter-governmental organisations, civic and private organisations are also increasingly involved in data gathering and dissemination in the area of gender equality. Their work played an especially prominent role during the last decade when numerous new initiatives and projects were established, either solely or partly focusing on empirical data gathering on gender equality issues. In the following paragraphs, we will outline some of the significant initiatives without being exhaustive or offering an in-detail analysis of these efforts (which would require a report on its own).

---

26. https://www.ilo.org/global/topics/equality-and-discrimination/gender-equality/lang--en/index.htm

27. https://www.unfpa.org/swop

28. https://www.unodc.org/unodc/gender/index.html

29. https://www.fao.org/gender/en/

30. https://www.itu.int/en/equals/pages/default.aspx

31. http://ec.europa.eu/justice/gender-equality/gender-decision-making/index_en.htm

32. http://www.gemconsortium.org/

33. http://www.ipu.org/wmn-e/classif.htm

Equal Measures 2030

Equal Measures 2030[34] is an independent civil society and private sector-led partnership that connects data and evidence with advocacy and action, helping to fuel progress towards gender equality. Equal Measures 2030 provides Gender Advocates Data Hub[35], which they describe as the go-to resource for data, visualisations and impact stories showcasing data-driven advocacy on gender equality issues across the Sustainable Development Goals (SDG). Visitors can explore the state of gender equality across 129 countries, covering 95% of the world's girls and women.

The partnership produces the SDG Gender Index that provides a snapshot of where the world stands linked to the vision of gender equality set forth by the 2030 Agenda. The 2019 version of this Index[36] measures the state of gender equality aligned to 14 of the 17 Sustainable Development Goals (SDGs) in 129 countries in five regions and 51 issues ranging from health, gender-based violence, climate change, decent work and others.

Data 2x

Data2X[37], an initiative announced in 2012, uses data to advance gender equality and women's empowerment. The United Nations Foundation leads an initiative with support from the William and Flora Hewlett Foundation, the Bill & Melinda Gates Foundation and the Clinton Foundation. Data2x has two key goals, and both focused on empirical data on gender equality:

34. https://data.em2030.org/

35. https://data.em2030.org/

36. https://data.em2030.org/wp-content/uploads/2019/07/
    EM2030_2019_Global_Report_English_WEB.pdf

37. http://www.unfoundation.org/what-we-do/issues/women-and-population/data2x.html

First, it helps build the case and mobilise action for gender data. In particular, through their research, advocacy, and communications, we make gender data central to global efforts to achieve gender equality. Secondly, they aim to strengthen the production and use of gender data. From traditional data systems to new data sources, they push to ensure that data collection methods are unbiased and gender-sensitive.

Since its establishment, this initiative has gone a long way in identifying the gaps in available reliable empirical data on gender equality around the world. Probably due to their strong political and financial support, they have also generated a lot of interest in empirical data generation and validation in this area. In addition, they are publishing some of the most illuminating and reader-friendly overviews of the current state of affairs in the area of empirical data on gender equality, both globally and regionally, that we would recommend for reading. One of such reports, produced in collaboration with the Open Data Watch[38] initiative, is available here[39] (Open Data Watch, and UNESCAP, 2019). Finally, they offer an extensive resource hub[40] with datasets, publications, case studies, manuals, toolkits, and other materials on various topics directly relevant to gender equality.

PARIS21

The Partnership in Statistics for Development in the 21st Century[41] (PARIS21) promotes the better use and production of statistics throughout the developing world. Since its establishment in 1999, PARIS21 has successfully developed a worldwide network of

---

38. https://opendatawatch.com/

39. https://opendatawatch.com/wp-content/uploads/2021/Publications/Bridging-the-Gap-Gender-Data-Asia-Pacific-Technical-Report.pdf

40. https://data2x.org/resource-center/

41. https://paris21.org/

statisticians, policymakers, analysts, and development practitioners committed to evidence-based decision making.

As part of its collaboration with UN Women[42], PARIS21 developed a comprehensive framework[43] to assess data and capacity gaps linked to gender statistics. The framework, aimed at national statistical offices, proposes methods, activities and tools for conducting assessments related to gender statistics to support the mainstreaming of gender statistics in national statistical systems (NSS).

Generation Equality Forum

The Generation Equality Forum[44] took place in Mexico City in March and Paris from 30 June – 2 July 2021. The Forum launched a 5-year action journey to achieve irreversible progress towards gender equality, founded on a series of concrete, ambitious and transformative actions, including $40 Billion in financial commitments. In addition, the Forum developed the Global Acceleration Plan[45] – a global road map for gender equality that aims to fulfil the promise of the Beijing Platform for Action and achieve the Sustainable Development Goals. It involves every sector of society and calls for the collection of reliable, relevant and gender-specific data on all aspects of gender equality.

The Core Group[46] was the decision-making body for the Generation Equality Forum, co-chaired by UN Women, France, Mexico and two representatives from civil society (from Global North and Global South). The Core Group established a Multi-Stakeholder Steering

42. https://paris21.org/supporting-gender-statistics

43. https://paris21.org/node/3286

44. https://forum.generationequality.org/forum

45. https://forum.generationequality.org/sites/default/files/2021-06/
    UNW%20-%20GAP%20Report%20-%20EN.pdf

46. https://forum.generationequality.org/core-group

Committee[47] comprising members from civil society, Member States, the private sector, and other stakeholders to contribute to the Forum's design, planning, and implementation.

In summary, the state of global evidence on gender equality can be described as varied, insufficient, and growing at a much faster pace in the recent decade. Many institutional players are involved in providing their contribution, often in their specialised research fields. Recent years also show marked improvement in the coordination of the empirical efforts across various organisations, spearheaded by producing the UN's SDGs. Notably, several private-public partnerships have emerged, best exemplified by the Data 2x initiative, which invigorates efforts to produce better-quality data and coordinate them across various governmental and non-governmental actors and stakeholders. Yet, as said, despite all of this effort, significant gaps in the empirical evidence on gender equality remain. We will discuss them in the final section of this report.

---

47. https://forum.generationequality.org/multi-stakeholder-steering-committee

7. Gaps in empirical evidence on Gender Equality

Development funders and policymakers use data to guide their investments and governance priorities. However, when the available data does not accurately capture the realities of women's and men's lives, funding is inefficiently allocated, and policies may not meet the needs of the people they should serve. Indeed, some consider the underachievement of the United Nations Millennium Development Goals (MDGs) – including MDG 5 on gender equality to improve maternal health – due to the lack of indicators to track progress (Leadership Council of the Sustainable Development Solutions Network 2015). In response, the Sustainable Development Goals (SDGs) that have replaced the MDGs have more indicators than any previous global development goals. Yet, we currently lack data for 80% of the gender equality indicators across the SDGs (UN Women 2017). As a result, UN Women has called for collecting sex-disaggregated data to ensure that women, girls and their needs are visible (UN Women 2018, 46). However, even a few years ago, only 37% of the 126 countries surveyed by the UN Statistics Division had a coordinating body to ensure the collection of sex-disaggregated statistics (Gender Statistics, UNESC 2013). This situation – the lack of sex-disaggregated statistics – is commonly referred to as the gender data gap.

The 2019 Report of the Secretary-General on the progress towards the SDGs confirmed that, despite the 2030 Agenda's new impetus for statistics, there remain several challenges related to the set of indicators for SDG 5 (gender equality) and other gender indicators across various SDGs (UN, 2019). The report stressed that "there is simply no way that the world can achieve the 17 Sustainable Development Goals without also achieving gender equality and the empowerment of women and girls" (UN, 2019).

Gaps in data at the country level have significant implications for national progress monitoring on the SDGs and regional and global monitoring, as these aggregates are ultimately derived from country-level data. Only 10 (19%) of the 54 gender-specific indicators are produced with enough regularity to be classified as Tier I by the IAEG-SDGs. Only two indicators under SDG 5 are currently classified as Tier I (see **Figure 23**). The remaining three gender-specific indicators (6%) have components spanning multiple tiers.

Many gender-specific SDG indicators cover areas where data production methodologies are undefined or emerging. However, even in well-established methods, official statistics are often missing. Country-level gender data gaps impede national, regional and global monitoring of SDGs progress. As of April 2020, only 16 of the 53 gender-specific indicators (30%) are produced with enough regularity to be classified as Tier I by the IAEG-SDGs, meaning that not enough data is available to monitor progress across all regions.

Figure 23: Gender-specific SDG indicators by tier classification

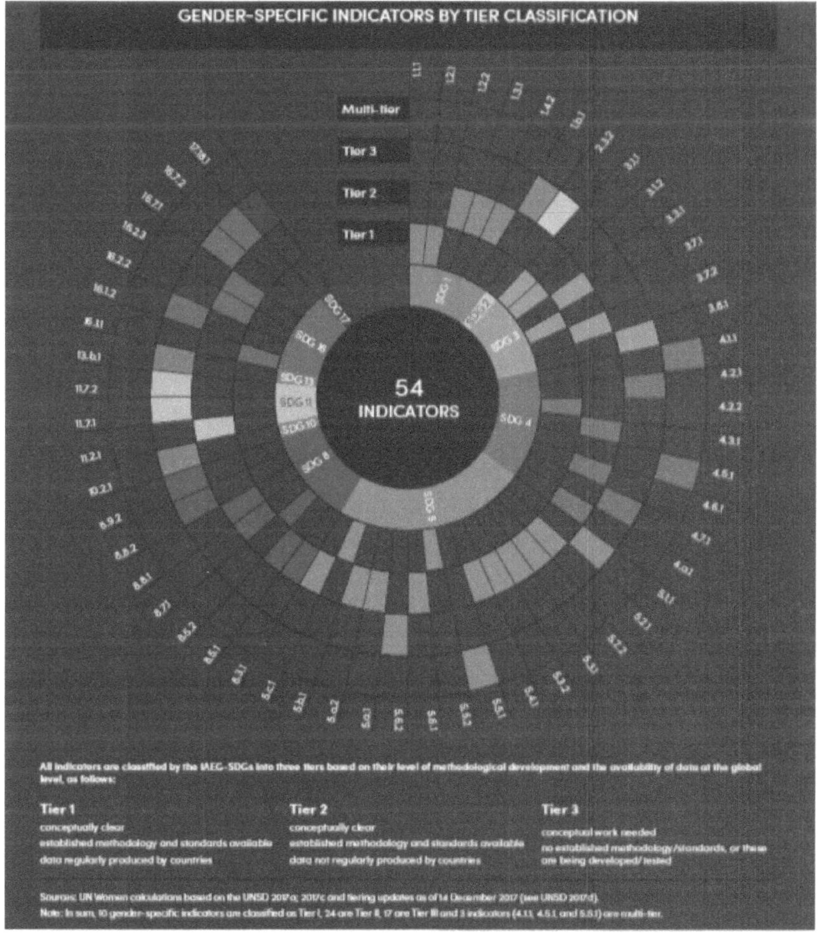

Source: UN Women, 2018.

The mismatch between data availability and data demand in the context of the SDGs is a shared concern for wealthy and developing countries alike – as one senior national statistician explained: "The SDGs have made us all data poor". Demographic and Health Surveys (DHS) and Multiple Indicator Cluster Surveys (MICS) are essential sources for comparable statistics across developing countries on a wide range of areas related to population, health and nutrition. But similar instruments do not readily exist in developed countries. That does not mean that data cannot be extracted from other surveys for these countries, but more effort will be needed to harmonise the information across countries.

Consequences of gender data gaps

The absence of adequate data can impede progress in creating informed and effective policies. Gender data gaps can be linked to three challenges[1]:

Weak policy space, and legal and financial environments, are barriers to progress

In many countries, the production of gender statistics is not specified in statistics laws and policies. As a result, the sector is under-prioritised and under-funded in national budgets.

Technical and financial challenges limit the production of gender statistics

Areas such as violence against women, sexual and reproductive health and rights, unpaid care and domestic work are significant to measure but are under-resourced. Also at risk are emerging areas, such as gender and poverty, gender pay gaps and women's participation in decision-making, where a lot more methodological work is needed.

Lack of access to data and limited capacity of users to use gender statistics to inform policies

Available data not shared in user-friendly formats impedes its use in informing evidence-based advocacy in decision-making. When data is not used to inform policy and advocacy, it leads to low demand, reducing the incentive to produce new gender statistics.

Main aspects of gender data gaps

Although the gender data gap is sometimes referred to as a single, homogeneous issue, it contains several distinct aspects that jointly contribute to its size and severity. **Figure 24** shows data gaps across some critical issues (the list is not exhaustive).

Figure 24: Data gaps across various indicators and aspects of data

	Type of gap			
	Lacking coverage across countries and/or regular country production	Lacking international standards	Lacking complexity (information across domains)	Lacking granularity (large detailed datasets allowing for disaggregation)
Health				
Maternal morbidity/mortality	■			■
Women's excess disease burdens	■			
Violence against women	■		■	
Mental health	■		■	■
Adolescent health	■		■	■
Utilization of health services by women	■			■
Education				
Learning outcomes	■	■		
Excluded girls	■	■		
Transition rates	■			
Economic Opportunities				
Unpaid work	■			
Informal employment	■			
Earnings and opportunity cost of paid work	■	■		
Conditions of migrant workers	■	■		
Employment mobility	■	■	■	■
Entrepreneurship	■		■	■
Asset ownership	■		■	■
Productivity in agriculture	■	■	■	■
Access to financial services	■			
Access to child care	■	■	■	■
Access to ICT (mobile phones & Internet)	■	■	■	■
Political Participation				
Representation in local governance, political organizations & the professions	■	■		
National identity documentation	■			■
Voter registration and turnout	■	■		
Human Security				
Conflict-related mortality and morbidity	■			■
Forcibly displaced and migrant profiles	■			■
Impact of conflict on gender variables; women's adaptive responses to conflict	■		■	■
Conflict-related sexual and gender-based violence	■		■	■
Women's participation in peace and security processes	■	■	■	■

Source: Buvinic et al. (2014). Mapping Gender Data Gaps, data2x.org.

Data availability

Data availability is the crucial determinant of gender data gaps. For example, the problems with data availability might relate to the lack of national or international measures, lack of sex disaggregation, non-conformity to standards, etc. (**Figure 25**). However, it is important to stress that data availability, although a necessary condition for filling the data gaps, is not a sufficient condition. Indeed, in the following paragraphs, we will list a selection of other data aspects that also need to be taken into account when deciding whether or not specific data could be used as a valid indicator of gender equality.

Figure 25: Availability of data in international and national datasets

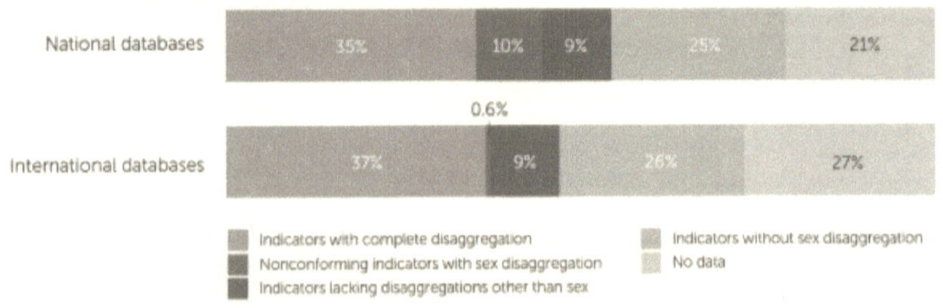

Source: Open Data Watch, 2021.

Data quality

Data quality depends on many factors: whether the data were properly collected and recorded; in the case of the survey data, whether the sample frame was well constructed and of sufficient size; whether the construction of the indicator conformed to recognised standards and definitions, whether the measure is reliable and valid, etc. At this moment, it is sufficient to say that all of the discussed aspects in the following paragraphs are related to data quality, either directly or indirectly.

Adherence to standards

Adherence to international standards is documented in the metadata inventory recorded as part of the assessments. Indicators whose descriptions did not match their SDG definition or their description in the UN Women's Turning Promises into Action were classified as "non-conforming" with their disaggregations recorded (UN Women, 2019) (**Figure 26**).

Figure 26: Number of countries meeting gender data standards between 2015 and 2019

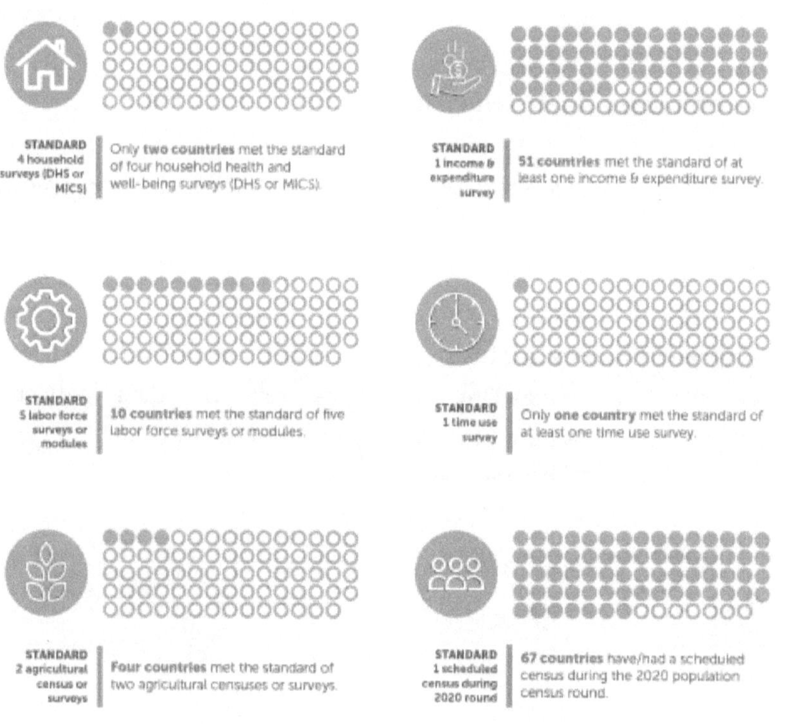

Source: Open Data Watch, 2021.

Timeliness

The timeliness and frequency of data are even more significant issues. Only 24% of the data available for gender-specific indicators are from 2010 or later (**Figure 27** below). Many national statistics are based on national censuses that usually occur only once in a decade. Likewise, most national and international surveys used for gathering gender data are administered across relatively long intervals or 3, 4 or 5 years. In addition, there is usually a long period of data gathering, quality checks and cleaning, analyses and integration, which can in some cases add an extra year or two until a given data point is included in a global indicator. All of this is problematic in an increasingly fast-changing global environment.

Lack of longitudinal/trend data

Reliance on repeated cross-sectional surveys means that longitudinal dynamics are rarely captured, for example, the long-term psychological effects of violence and harassment. Globally, only 17% of the gender-specific indicators with data have information for two or more points in time, allowing for trend analysis (**Figure 27**). That suggests that many gender-specific indicators rely on data collection mechanisms that were ad hoc or one-off exercises and not integrated into national statistical plans and strategies.

Figure 27: Availability of data for the 54 gender-specific indicators, by country, region and globally, 2000-2015

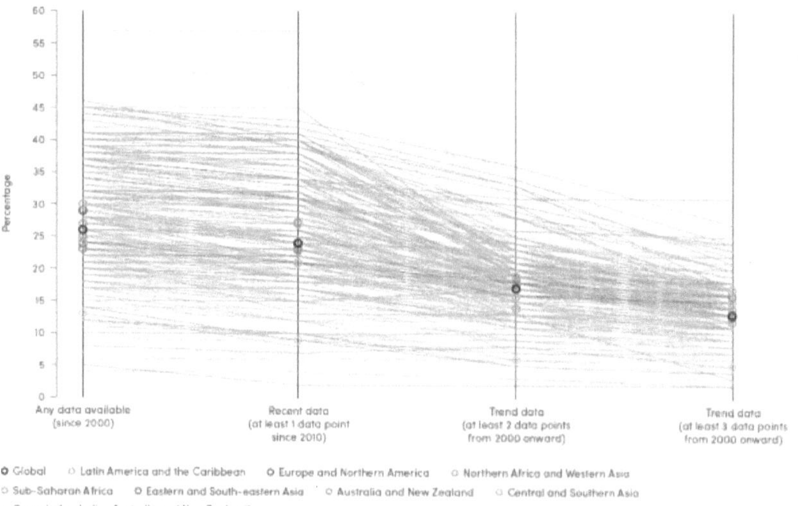

Source: UN Women (2019) calculations based on the assessment of data availability for all 54 gender-specific indicators and their sub-components across a total of 208 countries and areas/territories.

Disaggregation

The shift from the MDG to the SDG era has increased the demand for disaggregated and nuanced data. However, basic sex disaggregation remains an issue. There is also an unmet need for multiple disaggregations covering income, age, race, ethnicity, location (urban/rural), indigenous status, migration status, and disability.

Disaggregation remains a crucial challenge across sectors as most data are collected at the household rather than individual level. Across domains, sex disaggregation is not explicitly called for in monitoring many gender-relevant SDG indicators. Furthermore, even where data is disaggregated by sex, in-depth gender analyses are not always undertaken.

     MILOS KANKARAS

Data comparability

Good quality statistics enable policymakers to make important decisions, assess their country's position relative to other countries, and anticipate or react to trends. If the underlying data and methods are flawed, the policy responses will be similarly inadequate. Gender biases embedded in the concepts, definitions and classifications used, the way of asking questions, how the samples are designed and calculated for population surveys, and how data are collected hurt the quality of the data and reliability of the information they intend to convey. Differences in sources, definitions, concepts, survey population samples, and methods compromise the data's comparability across countries and time. Yet, such flaws and biases remain pervasive, affecting the quality of gender statistics.

Restricted sampling

Restricted sampling means we know most about women of reproductive age (15-49) but little about children, younger adolescents, or older women. Sampling issues are frequent in the empirical survey research where researchers often do not have enough resources to reach all subpopulations of their target audiences. The resulting sampling biases can substantially reduce the validity of obtained populational estimates. This problem is additionally emphasised by the fact that those hard-to-reach and hard-to-sample subgroups of the population are often the ones that are in the direst state regarding their status and rights, including their gender equality rights.

Different availability across domains

There is enormous variability in the availability of gender data across different domains. Globally, close to 80% of countries regularly produce sex-disaggregated statistics on mortality, labour force participation, and education and training. Educational indicators, followed by health, lead the way in terms of clarity, comparability and country coverage. On the other hand, less than a third of countries disaggregate statistics by gender on informal employment, entrepreneurship (ownership and management of a firm or business), violence against women, and unpaid work. Availability and coverage in these domains are poor, and this is especially the case for economic indicators. A list of gender data availability across various fields is available in **Appendix 3**.

The compartmentalisation of gender equality aspects

The SDG framework, like the MDGs, compartmentalise gender within specific goals and targets, often ignoring linkages across goals – for example, how environmental degradation impacts women's economic opportunities. That has spillover effects on how gender equality research and programming are conceptualised and funded.

The challenge of technical knowledge

The uptake and use of gender data for designing policies and programs are challenged in translating statistics to less technical audiences. In other words, even when good quality data are gathered in a comparative way globally, the job is not done. Therefore, a focused and consistent effort is needed to present data in a clear, concise and user-friendly manner so that its meaning and message is transmitted to the broad audience of diverse stakeholders worldwide.

Difficulties in obtaining legal data

Laws and policies, particularly those related to marriage, property, and labour rights, influence health, education, and economic outcomes for women are essential aspects of gender equality. However, comprehensive information on policies related to women is difficult to obtain. Therefore, this report reviews the databases that help document laws and policies affecting women's outcomes. Additional efforts to expand coverage and improve the robustness of these databases are warranted to round out the availability of policy-relevant data on women.

Progress is being made

When discussing the issue of gender data gaps, it is important to point out that there is some progress in closing these gaps. For example, although several indicators in the SDG 5 domain (gender equality) have been initially classified in tier 3 (indicating that they cannot be reliably monitored), all of the SDG 5 indicators are currently classified either in tier 1 or 2. **Figure 28** presents a more detailed overview of the progress in closing the gender data gaps across various indicators in recent years (based on Open Data Watch and UNESCAP, 2019).

Figure 28: Progress in gender data gaps across various gender equality indicators

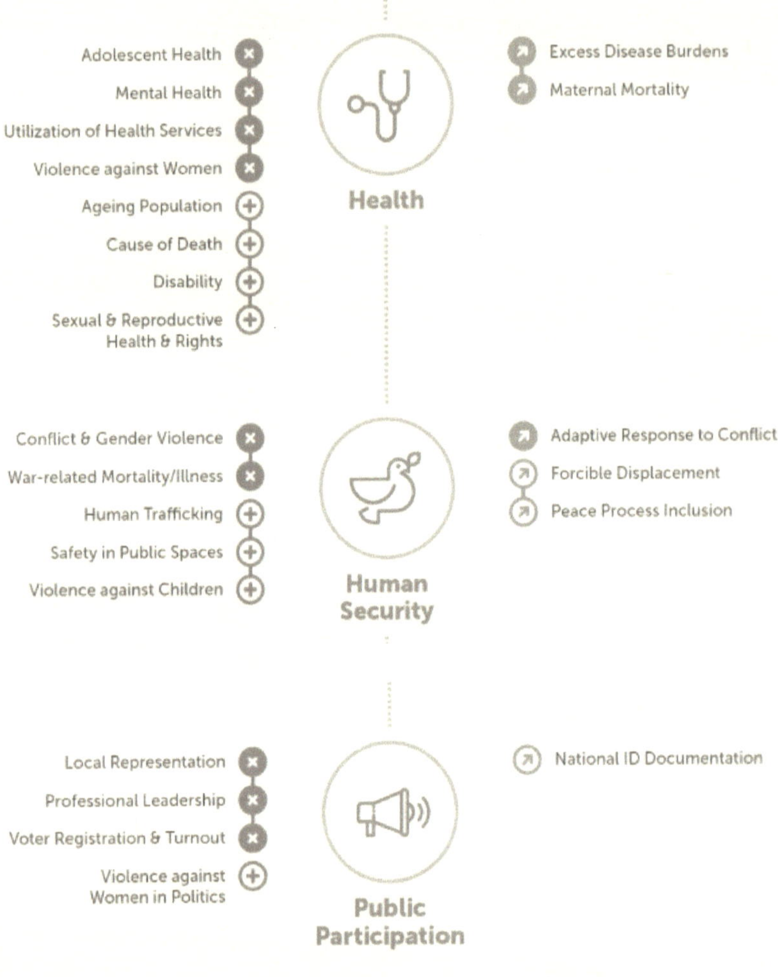

Source: Data2x (2021), Data2x.org/appingGenderDataGaps.

Concluding discussion

In the end, we would like to make two critical points that are often missing in available examinations and overviews of the gender data gaps, mainly in discussions concerning the SDG framework.

Measurability should not subdue the principle of data relevance

The central missing question in these discussions is the relevance of the selected indicators of gender equality in describing the real-life manifestation and lived experiences of gender equality. It is often assumed that 54 gender-specific indicators in the SDG framework account for the entirety of the gender equality aspects, or at least for the majority of them. But this is so far from the truth, in my opinion. It is enough, for example, to read that the only indicator of gender equality in the area of digital technology and, indeed, technology as a whole is whether or not a person owns a mobile phone. One does not need to dwell much about all the vastly different situations two persons who own a mobile phone can (and inevitably will) have in terms of the access to and use of (digital) technologies. Having an indicator on one aspect of life does not necessarily mean that that indicator accounts for the entirety of lived experiences or inequalities occurring in this aspect.

What makes the problem worse in this sense is that there is a clear bias towards the inclusion of measurable quantitative indicators. There are clear, practical reasons for doing this. The indicators that can be more easily quantified and measured allow easier, cheaper, more standardised data gathering and analyses, comparisons, and index constructions. However, although quantitative indicators often validly reflect some aspects of the relevant reality, they are not comprehensive in accounting for the entirety of lived experiences of gender inequality. One could even claim that these indicators might not capture the core of subjectively perceived gender inequality, which may be the most critical aspect of gender equality from the people's point of view. That is why some researchers and activists suggest that the burgeoning demands to produce evidence of impact constitute a 'measurement obsession' (Liebowitz and Zwingel 2014) and that the focus is overly quantitative. They have also questioned the extent to which available data is 'fit for purpose', noting that it is incredibly challenging to capture the myriad ways in which inequalities are manifested and sustained (Bradshaw, Chant, and Linneker 2017).

The solution is certainly not to stop collecting quantitative data but rather to be aware of the gaps in these data and their shortcomings. Likewise, much more needs to be done to capture the lived experiences of women and girls. We need to be aware of what we are not capturing before we can do something about it. We generally don't see that that is the case currently across these institutions and stakeholders. To conclude, it is not true that we have one-third of the data to estimate the global degree of gender equality, as indicated in several publications, including those by UN organisations. The actual proportion of relevant available data is much less. We estimate that there are less than 10% of comparable, relevant, and timely data on gender equality across the world. A lot of work needs to be done, and hopefully, Minderoo can make its own contribution to this field.

A broader data value chain should be considered, and in it, there is the widest data gap of all

It is essential to realise that the empirical data on gender equality are part of a broader system or network that some refer to the data value chain (see Open Data Watch & UNESCAP, 2019). The concept of data value chain breaks down the process through which data move from production to use, covering the four stages of collection, publication, uptake, and impact (**Figure 29**). The collection stage involves gathering raw data through surveys and other sources and preparing it for analysis. The publication stage consists of analysing raw data to make data publicly available. Finally, the uptake stage relies on data intermediaries to allow users to access and use available data.

The impact stage covers the ultimate impacts that improve the lives of women and girls. Many stakeholders cover multiple stages of the data value chain. However, most focus on either collecting or publishing data and fewer work to increase the uptake and impact of gender data among users. And few stakeholders were found that focus on impacts of gender data to directly improve the lives of women and girls, as the scope of this mapping exercise was on stakeholders that provided support for data itself.

Figure 29: Number of stakeholders providing support for each stage of the global data value chain

Source: Open Data Watch, 2021.

This broader framework on the role and use of gender data is critical in understanding the most significant gaps and the key benefits of obtained data. In addition, such a framework allows for a better allocation of resources and activities across various stages to achieve the most significant impact with the available means. For example, the overview of the data presented in **Figure 29** clearly shows that more efforts should be made in the last stages of the value chain, especially in the 'Impact' stage, where the fewest stakeholders are engaged. The fact is that the value and effectiveness of all stages directly depend on the successful administration of this last stage.

I would even go a step further and suggest that maybe the central gender data gap not discussed in any of the reviewed reports is related to this last impact stage. There is very little to no solid empirical evidence on which policy initiatives work and which don't work, and what are the factors and contextual characteristics that contribute to or influence the final outcome. And without such knowledge, we are very far from translating our available gender data into effective policy action. So, in my opinion, one of the most effective ways in which Minderoo could contribute to the global issues on gender equality would be to help build better evidence depository of the factors contributing to the success or failure of various policy initiatives in this area.

References

Belingheri P, Chiarello F, Fronzetti Colladon A, Rovelli P (2021) Twenty years of gender equality research: A scoping review based on a new semantic indicator. PLoS ONE 16(9): e0256474. https://doi.org/10.1371/journal.pone.0256474

Bradshaw, S., Chant, S. & Linneker, B. (2017). Gender and poverty: what we know, don't know, and need to know for Agenda 2030, Gender, Place & Culture, 24:12, 1667-1688, DOI: 10.1080/0966369X.2017.1395821

Buvinic, M., Furst-Nichols, R. & Koolwal, G. (2014). Mapping Gender Data Gaps, Data2x. https://data2x.org/wp-content/uploads/2019/05/Data2X_MappingGenderDataGaps_FullReport.pdf

Data2X (2021). Mapping a Gender Data Gaps: an Infographic. Data2x. data2x.org/MappingGenderDataGaps.

Liebowitz, D. & Zwingel, S. (2014). Gender Equality Oversimplified: Using CEDAW to Counter the Measurement Obsession. International Studies Review. 16. 10.1111/misr.12139.

OECD (2012), *Closing the Gender Gap: Act Now*, OECD Publishing, Paris, http://dx.doi.org/10.1787/9789264179370-en.

OECD (2018), Survey on Private Philanthropy for Development 2013-15: Data Questionnaire, www.oecd.org/dac/financingsustainable-development/ development-finance-standards/beyond-   oda-foundations.htm

OECD (2019a), SIGI 2019 Global Report: Transforming Challenges into Opportunities, Social Institutions

and Gender Index, OECD Publishing, Paris. https://doi.org/10.1787/bc56d212-en

OECD (2019b), OECD International Development Statistics: Creditor Reporting System (database), http://www.oecd.org/dac/stats/idsonline.htm

Open Data Watch (2021). State of Gender Financing 2021, https://data2x.org/wp-content/uploads/2021/ 05/State-of-Gender-Data-Financing-2021_FINAL.pdf

Open Data Watch and UNESCAP (2019). Bridging the Gap: Mapping Gender Data Availability in Asia and the Pacific, https://data2x.org/wp-content/uploads/2019/06/ Bridging-the-Gap-Technical-Report-Web-Ready.pdf

UN (1995). Beijing Declaration and Platform of Action, adopted at the Fourth World Conference on Women, 27 October 1995. A/CONF.177/20 and A/CONF.177/20/ Add.1.

UN (2015a). The Millennium Development Goals Report 2015. New York: United Nations.

UN (2015b). "Gender Statistics Manual: Integrating a Gender Perspective into Statistics." Accessed 8 November 2017. http://unstats.un.org/unsd/genderstatmanual/.

UN (2017). The Sustainable Development Goals Report 2017. New York: United Nations.

UN (2019). Progress towards the Sustainable Development Goals : report of the Secretary-General, https://digitallibrary.un.org/record/3810131?ln=en

UN CEDAW (United Nations Committee on the Elimination of Discrimination against Women), (1989). General Recommendation No. 9 on Statistical Data Concerning the Situation of Women. A/44/38

UN CSW (United Nations Commission on the Status of Women). 2013. "Elimination and Prevention of All Forms of Violence against Women and Girls: Agreed Conclusions." E/2013/27-E/CN.6/2013/11.

UN DESA (United Nations Department of Economic and Social Affairs) (2019). Minimum Set of Gender Indicators, https://doi.org/10.18356/e16af645-en

UNDP (2020). Human Development Report: The next frontier Human development and the Anthropocene.

UN Economic and Social Council (2013). Gender Statistics, Report of the Secretary-General. E/CN.3/2013/1.

UN Women (2018). Turning promises into action: Gender equality in the 2030 Agenda for Sustainable Development https://www.unwomen.org/en/digital-library/publications/2018/2/gender-equality-in-the-2030- agenda-for-sustainable-development-2018

UN Women (2019). Progress of the World's Women 2019-2020: Families in a Changing World. https://doi.org/10.18356/696a9392-en

UN Women (2021). Progress on the Sustainable Development Goals: The gender snapshot 2021, https://www.unwomen.org/sites/default/files/Headquarters/Attachments/Sections/Library/Publications/2021/Progress-on-the-Sustainable-Development-Goals-The-gender-snapshot- 2021-en.pdf

UNECE, (2015). "Indicators of Gender Equality", https://unece.org/sites/default/files/ 2022-02/ECE_CES_37_WEB.pdf

World Bank (2011). World development report 2012: Gender equality and development. Washington, DC.

World Bank (2015). World Bank Group Gender Strategy (FY16-23): Gender Equality, Poverty Reduction and Inclusive Growth. World Bank, Washington, DC. https://openknowledge.worldbank.org/ handle/10986/23425

World Bank (2016). World Development Report 2016: Digital Dividends. Washington, DC.

World Bank (2019). The Little Data Book on Gender 2019. World Bank, Washington, DC. © World Bank.

https://openknowledg e.worldbank.org/handle/ 10986/ 31689

World Economic Forum (2021). Global Gender Gap Report 2021, https://www3.weforum.org/docs/ WEF_GGGR_2021.pdf

Appendix 1: Core Provisions of CEDAW

Article 1 defines discrimination against women in the following terms:

Any distinction, exclusion or restriction made on the basis of sex which has the effect or purpose of impairing or nullifying the recognition, enjoyment or exercise by women, irrespective of their marital status, on a basis of equality of men and women, of human rights and fundamental freedoms in the political, economic, social, cultural, civil or any other field.

Article 2 mandates that states parties ratifying the Convention declare intent to enshrine gender equality into their domestic legislation, repeal all discriminatory provisions in their laws, and enact new provisions to guard against discrimination against women. States ratifying the Convention must also establish tribunals and public institutions to guarantee women effective protection against discrimination, and take steps to eliminate all forms of discrimination practiced against women by individuals, organisations, and enterprises.

Article 3 requires states parties to guarantee basic human rights and fundamental freedoms to women "on a basis of equality with men" through the "political, social, economic, and cultural fields."

Article 4 notes that "[a]doption...of special measures aimed at accelerating de facto equality between men and women shall not be considered discrimination." It adds that special protection for maternity[1] is not regarded as gender discrimination.

---

1. https://en.wikipedia.org/wiki/Maternity

Article 5 requires states parties to take measures to seek to eliminate prejudices and customs based on the idea of the inferiority or the superiority of one sex or on stereotyped[2] role for men and women[3]. It also mandates the states parties "[t]o ensure...the recognition of the common responsibility of men and women in the upbringing and development of their children."

Article 6 obliges states parties to "take all appropriate measures, including legislation, to suppress all forms of trafficking in women[4] and exploitation of prostitution[5] of women."

Article 7 guarantees women equality in political and public life with a focus on equality in voting[6], participation in government, and participation in "non-governmental organisations and associations concerned with the public and political life of the country."

Article 8 provides that states parties will guarantee women's equal "opportunity to represent their Government at the international level and to participate in the work of international organisations[7]."

Article 9 mandates state parties to "grant women equal rights with men to acquire, change or retain their nationality[8]" and equal rights "with respect to the nationality of their children."

Article 10 necessitates equal opportunity in education for female students and encourages coeducation[9]. It also provides equal access

---

2. https://en.wikipedia.org/wiki/Stereotype

3. https://en.wikipedia.org/wiki/Gender_role

4. https://en.wikipedia.org/wiki/Trafficking_in_women

5. https://en.wikipedia.org/wiki/Forced_prostitution

6. https://en.wikipedia.org/wiki/Suffrage

7. https://en.wikipedia.org/wiki/International_organizations

8. https://en.wikipedia.org/wiki/Nationality

9. https://en.wikipedia.org/wiki/Mixed-sex_education

to athletics, scholarships and grants as well as requires "reduction in female students' drop out rates."

Article 11 outlines the right to work[10] for women as "an unalienable right[11] of all human beings." It requires equal pay for equal work[12], the right to social security[13], paid leave[14] and maternity leave[15] "with pay or with comparable social benefits[16] without loss of former employment, seniority or social allowances." Dismissal on the grounds of maternity, pregnancy[17] or status of marriage shall be prohibited with sanction.

Article 12 creates the obligation of states parties to "take all appropriate measures to eliminate discrimination against women in the field of healthcare in order to ensure...access to health care services, including those related to family planning[18]."

Article 13 guarantees equality to women "in economic and social life," especially with respect to "the right to family benefits, the right to bank loans, mortgages and other forms of financial credit, and the right to participate in recreational activities, sports and all aspects of cultural life."

Article 14 provides protections for rural women and their special problems, ensuring the right of women to participate in development programs, "to have access to adequate health care facilities," "to

---

10. https://en.wikipedia.org/wiki/Right_to_work

11. https://en.wikipedia.org/wiki/Unalienable_rights

12. https://en.wikipedia.org/wiki/Equal_pay_for_equal_work

13. https://en.wikipedia.org/wiki/Right_to_social_security

14. https://en.wikipedia.org/wiki/Paid_leave

15. https://en.wikipedia.org/wiki/Maternity_leave

16. https://en.wikipedia.org/wiki/Social_benefits

17. https://en.wikipedia.org/wiki/Pregnancy

18. https://en.wikipedia.org/wiki/Family_planning

participate in all community activities," "to have access to agricultural credit" and "to enjoy adequate living conditions."

Article 15 obliges states parties to guarantee "women equality with men before the law," including "a legal capacity[19] identical to that of men." It also accords "to men and women the same rights with regard to the law relating to the movement of persons[20] and the freedom to choose their residence and domicile."

Article 16 prohibits "discrimination against women in all matters relating to marriage and family relations." In particular, it provides men and women with "the same right to enter into marriage, the same right freely to choose a spouse," "the same rights and responsibilities during marriage[21] and at its dissolution," "the same rights and responsibilities as parents," "the same rights to decide freely and responsibly on the number and spacing of their children," "the same personal rights as husband and wife, including the right to choose a family name, a profession and an occupation" "the same rights for both spouses in respect of the ownership, acquisition, management, administration, enjoyment and disposition of property, whether free of charge or for a valuable consideration."

Articles 17 - 24 These articles describe the composition and procedures of the CEDAW Committee, like the hierarchical structure and rules and regulations of systematic procedure of the relationship between CEDAW and national and international legislation and the obligation of States to take all steps necessary to implement CEDAW in full form.

Articles 25 - 30 (Administration of CEDAW)

---

19. https://en.wikipedia.org/wiki/Capacity_(law)

20. https://en.wikipedia.org/wiki/Freedom_of_movement

21. https://en.wikipedia.org/wiki/Marriage_law

These articles describe the general administrative procedures concerning enforcement of CEDAW, ratification and entering reservations of concerned states.

Appendix 2: Beijing Platform for Action – List of domains and objectives

Women and poverty diagnosis

- **Strategic objective A.1.** Review, adopt and maintain macroeconomic policies and development strategies that address the needs and efforts of women in poverty. Actions to be taken.
- **Strategic objective A.2.** Revise laws and administrative practices to ensure women's equal rights and access to economic resources. Actions to be taken.
- **Strategic objective A.3.** Provide women with access to savings and credit mechanisms and institutions. Actions to be taken.
- **Strategic objective A.4.** Develop gender-based methodologies and conduct research to address the feminisation of poverty. Actions to be taken.

Education and training of women diagnosis

- **Strategic objective B.1.** Ensure equal access to education. Actions to be taken.
- **Strategic objective B.2.** Eradicate illiteracy among women. Actions to be taken.
- **Strategic objective B.3.** Improve women's access to vocational training, science and technology, and continuing education. Actions to be taken.
- **Strategic objective B.4.** Develop non-discriminatory

education and training. Actions to be taken

- **Strategic objective B.5.** Allocate sufficient resources for and monitor the implementation of educational reforms. Actions to be taken.
- **Strategic objective B.6.** Promote lifelong education and training for girls and women. Actions to be taken.

Women and health diagnosis

- **Strategic objective C.1.** Increase women's access throughout the life cycle to appropriate, affordable and quality health care, information and related services. Actions to be taken.
- **Strategic objective C.2.** Strengthen preventive programmes that promote women's health. Actions to be taken.
- **Strategic objective C.3.** Undertake gender-sensitive initiatives that address sexually transmitted diseases, HIV/AIDS, and sexual and reproductive health issues. Actions to be taken.
- **Strategic objective C.4.** Promote research and disseminate information on women's health. Actions to be taken
- **Strategic objective C.5.** Increase resources and monitor follow-up for women's health. Actions to be taken.

Violence against women diagnosis

- **Strategic objective D.1.** Take integrated measures to prevent and eliminate violence against women. Actions to be taken.
- **Strategic objective D.2.** Study the causes and consequences of violence against women and the effectiveness of preventive measures. Actions to be taken.
- **Strategic objective D.3.** Eliminate trafficking in women and assist victims of violence due to prostitution and trafficking.

Actions to be taken.

Women and armed conflict diagnosis

- **Strategic objective E.1.** Increase the participation of women in conflict resolution at decision-making levels and protect women living in situations of armed and other conflicts or under foreign occupation. Actions to be taken.
- **Strategic objective E.2.** Reduce excessive military expenditures and control the availability of armaments. Actions to be taken.
- **Strategic objective E.3.** Promote non-violent forms of conflict resolution and reduce the incidence of human rights abuse in conflict situations. Actions to be taken.
- **Strategic objective E.4.** Promote women's contribution to fostering a culture of peace. Actions to be taken.
- **Strategic objective E.5.** Provide protection, assistance and training to refugee women, other displaced women in need of international protection and internally displaced women. Actions to be taken.
- **Strategic objective E.6.** Provide assistance to the women of the colonies and non-self-governing territories. Actions to be taken.

Women and the economy diagnosis

- **Strategic objective F.1.** Promote women's economic rights and independence, including access to employment, appropriate working conditions and control over economic resources. Actions to be taken.
- **Strategic objective F.2.** Facilitate women's equal access to resources, employment, markets and trade. Actions to be

taken.

- **Strategic objective F.3.** Provide business services, training and access to markets, information and technology, particularly to low-income women. Actions to be taken.
- **Strategic objective F.4.** Strengthen women's economic capacity and commercial networks. Actions to be taken.
- **Strategic objective F.5.** Eliminate occupational segregation and all forms of employment discrimination. Actions to be taken.
- **Strategic objective F.6.** Promote harmonisation of work and family responsibilities for women and men. Actions to be taken.

Women in power and decision-making diagnosis

- **Strategic objective G.1.** Take measures to ensure women's equal access to and full participation in power structures and decision-making. Actions to be taken.
- **Strategic objective G.2.** Increase women's capacity to participate in decision-making and leadership. Actions to be taken.

Institutional mechanism for the advancement of women diagnosis

- **Strategic objective H.1.** Create or strengthen national machineries and other governmental bodies. Actions to be taken.
- **Strategic objective H.2.** Integrate gender perspectives in legislation, public policies, programmes and projects. Actions to be taken.
- **Strategic objective H.3.** Generate and disseminate gender-disaggregated data and information for planning and

evaluation Actions to be taken.

Human rights of women diagnosis

- **Strategic objective I.1.** Promote and protect the human rights of women, through the full implementation of all human rights instruments, especially the Convention on the Elimination of All Forms of Discrimination against Women. Actions to be taken.
- **Strategic objective I.2.** Ensure equality and non-discrimination under the law and in practice. Actions to be taken.
- **Strategic objective I.3.** Achieve legal literacy. Actions to be taken.

Women and the media diagnosis

- **Strategic objective J.1.** Increase the participation and access of women to expression and decision-making in and through the media and new technologies of communication. Actions to be taken.
- **Strategic objective J.2.** Promote a balanced and non-stereotyped portrayal of women in the media. Actions to be taken.

Women and the environment diagnosis

- **Strategic objective K.1.** Involve women actively in environmental decision-making at all levels. Actions to be taken.
- **Strategic objective K.2.** Integrate gender concerns and perspectives in policies and programmes for sustainable

development. Actions to be taken.

- **Strategic objective K.3.** Strengthen or establish mechanisms at the national, regional, and international levels to assess the impact of development and environmental policies on women. Actions to be taken.

The girl-child diagnosis

- **Strategic objective L.1.** Eliminate all forms of discrimination against the girl-child. Actions to be taken.
- **Strategic objective L.2.** Eliminate negative cultural attitudes and practices against girls. Actions to be taken.
- **Strategic objective L.3.** Promote and protect the rights of the girl-child and increase awareness of her needs and potential. Actions to be taken.
- **Strategic objective L.4.** Eliminate discrimination against girls in education, skills development and training. Actions to be taken
- **Strategic objective L.5.** Eliminate discrimination against girls in health and nutrition. Actions to be taken.
- **Strategic objective L.6.** Eliminate the economic exploitation of child labour and protect young girls at work. Actions to be taken.
- **Strategic objective L.7.** Eradicate violence against the girl-child. Actions to be taken.
- **Strategic objective L.8.** Promote the girl-child's awareness of and participation in social, economic and political life. Actions to be taken.
- **Strategic objective L.9.** Strengthen the role of the family in improving the status of the girl-child. Actions to be taken.

Appendix 3: Production of gender statistics in different areas

Areas	Percentage of countries producing statistics		
	Regularly	*Irregularly*	*Not producing statistics*
Labour force	83.3	8.7	7.9
Informal employment	36.5	17.5	46.0
Unemployment	88.1	7.2	4.8
Poverty	70.6	14.3	15.1
Unpaid work	42.1	24.6	33.3
Satellite accounts	7.2	18.3	74.6
Entrepreneurship	27.8	19.1	53.2
Agriculture	44.4	19.1	36.5
Education and training	81.0	9.5	9.5
Power and decision-making	52.4	18.3	29.4
Media	15.1	19.8	65.1
Information and communications technology	38.9	20.6	40.5
Mortality	84.9	7.1	7.9
Morbidity	73.0	11.9	15.1
Disability	53.2	24.6	22.2
Access to health services	65.1	12.7	22.2
Sexual and reproductive health	65.9	14.3	19.8
Child marriage	39.7	11.1	49.2
Adolescent fertility	65.9	11.1	23.0
Violence against women	40.5	31.0	28.6
Access to clean water	37.3	17.5	45.2
Access to sanitation	38.9	16.7	44.4

Source: UN Economic and Social Council (2013). Gender Statistics, Report of the Secretary-General.

[1] https://data.unwomen.org/women-count

Don't miss out!

Visit the website below and you can sign up to receive emails whenever Milos Kankaras publishes a new book. There's no charge and no obligation.

https://books2read.com/r/B-A-GHFU-OINZB

BOOKS2READ

Connecting independent readers to independent writers.

Also by Milos Kankaras

Gender Equality
Policy and Research on Gender Equality: An Overview
The Global State of Gender Equality: An Overview of Empirical Findings
Violence Against Women and Girls: Effectiveness of Intervention Programs

About the Author

Dr Miloš Kankaraš is an experienced policy analyst, project manager and author with a rich track record in providing an empirical foundation for evidence-based public policy in international settings. He worked in academia before moving to some of the leading international organisations, where he examined issues ranging from education, skill development, social policy, working conditions, gender equality, quality of life, etc. Miloš published extensively in a variety of policy and research areas. He has an undergraduate degree in Psychology, graduate degrees in educational psychology and international social policy, and a PhD in the area of cross-cultural research.